North Devon

Walks

Compiled by
Sue Viccars

Dedication
In memory of Henry Williamson 1895–1977

Acknowledgements
Firstly I would like to thank Kevin Freeborn of Crimson Publishing for giving me the opportunity to spend my summer doing what I like best! Thanks too to my friend Brenda and my other half Stuart for their constant help and support, to Sarah Harrison, Countryside Officer at Devon County Council, and to Pat Edgar and Independent Hostels UK for help with accommodation on the North Devon coast.

Text:	Sue Viccars
Photography:	Sue Viccars
Editorial:	Ark Creative (UK) Ltd
Design:	Ark Creative (UK) Ltd

ISBN: 978-1-85458-553-0

While every care has been taken to ensure the accuracy of the route directions, the publishers cannot accept responsibility for errors or omissions, or for changes in details given. The countryside is not static: hedges and fences can be removed, field boundaries can alter, footpaths can be rerouted and changes in ownership can result in the closure or diversion of some concessionary paths. Also, paths that are easy and pleasant for walking in fine conditions may become slippery, muddy and difficult in wet weather, while stepping stones across rivers and streams may become impassable.

If you find an inaccuracy in either the text or maps, please write to Crimson Publishing at the address below.

Printed in Singapore. 1/11

First published in Great Britain 2011 by Crimson Publishing,
a division of:
Crimson Business Ltd,
Westminster House, Kew Road, Richmond, Surrey, TW9 2ND

www.totalwalking.co.uk

A catalogue record for this book is available from the British library.

Front cover: Rillage Point
Previous page: The lane from Balls Cross towards Merton

Contents

Approximate walk times

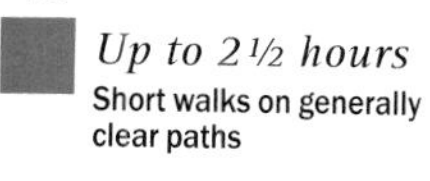

Up to 2½ hours
Short walks on generally clear paths

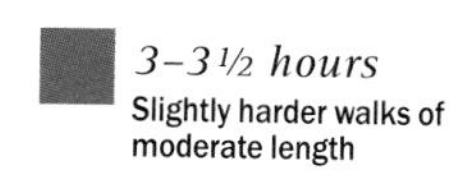

3–3½ hours
Slightly harder walks of moderate length

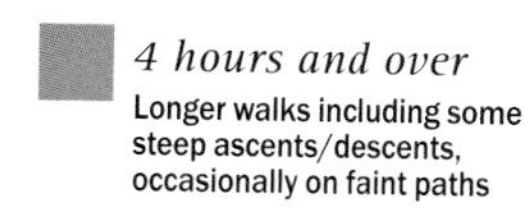

4 hours and over
Longer walks including some steep ascents/descents, occasionally on faint paths

The walk times are provided as a guide only and are calculated using an average walking speed of 2½mph (4km/h), adding one minute for each 10m (33ft) of ascent, and then rounding the result to the nearest half hour.

Walks are considered to be dog friendly unless specified.

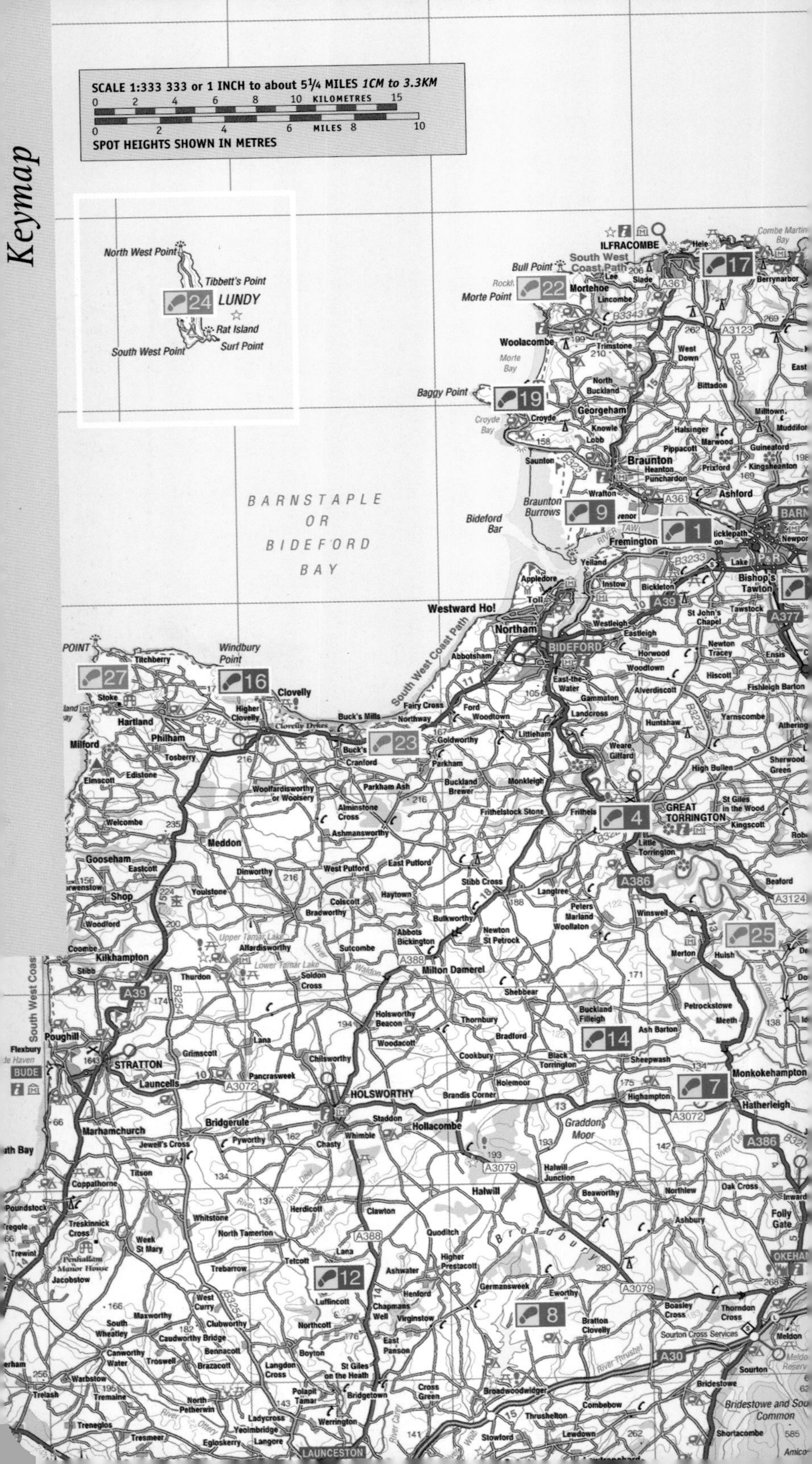

Keymap

SCALE 1:333 333 or 1 INCH to about 5¼ MILES *1CM to 3.3KM*

0 2 4 6 8 10 KILOMETRES 15

0 2 4 6 MILES 8 10

SPOT HEIGHTS SHOWN IN METRES

North West Point
Tibbett's Point
24 LUNDY
Rat Island
Surf Point
South West Point

BARNSTAPLE OR BIDEFORD BAY

ILFRACOMBE
17
Bull Point
22 Mortehoe
Morte Point
Woolacombe
Baggy Point
19
Croyde
Georgeham
Braunton
Braunton Burrows
9
1
Fremington
Bideford Bar
Appledore
Westward Ho!
Northam
BIDEFORD
Windbury Point
16 Clovelly
27 Hartland
23
4 GREAT TORRINGTON
25
14
7 Hatherleigh
STRATTON
BUDE
HOLSWORTHY
12
8
LAUNCESTON
OKEHAMPTON

BRISTOL CHANNEL
Foreland Point
South West Coast Path
Lynmouth
LYNTON
Countisbury
Porlock
MINEHEAD
Dunster
EXMOOR FOREST
EXMOOR NATIONAL PARK
EXMOOR
Brendon Common
Simonsbath
Exford
Withypool
Winsford
Dulverton
Tarr Steps
Molland Common
North Molton
SOUTH MOLTON
Chittlehampton
Bishop's Nympton
King's Nympton
Knowstone
Bampton
Oakford
TIVERTON
Cullompton
Chawleigh
Morchard Bishop
Copplestone
CREDITON
Bradninch
Silverton
Thorverton
EXETER
Exeter Airport
Topsham
Cheriton Bishop
Drewsteignton
South Zeal
Moretonhampstead
Chagford
Kennford
Shillingford St George
A39
A361
A396
A377
A3072
A30
A3124
M5
15
5
28
20
6
10
11
21
3
26
2

Walk	Page	Start	Nat. Grid Reference	Distance	Time	Height Gain
Arlington Court & Loxhore	56	Arlington Court	SS 611407	7 miles (11.3km)	3½ hrs	1,065ft (325m)
Baggy Point & Saunton Down	59	Croyde	SS 444392	7¼ miles (11.4km)	3½ hrs	1,065ft (325m)
Bampton & Morebath	36	Bampton	SS 956222	5½ miles (8.8km)	3 hrs	985ft (300m)
Berrynarbor & Widmouth Bay	53	Berrynarbor	SS 561466	7 miles (11.1km)	3½ hrs	1,265ft (385m)
Brampford Speke & the River Exe	14	Brampford Speke	SX 926982	3 miles (4.8km)	1½ hrs	n/a
Braunton Marsh & Burrows	30	Velator Quay, Braunton	SS 484354	6¼ miles (10km)	2½ hrs	n/a
Brownsham & Clovelly	50	Brownsham	SS 285259	6¾ miles (10.7km)	3½ hrs	1,525ft (465m)
Buck's Mills & Peppercombe	71	Parkham	SS 387210	7½ miles (12km)	4 hrs	1,490ft (455m)
Chulmleigh & Eggesford Forest	65	Chulmleigh	SS 686141	7½ miles (12.1km)	4 hrs	1,115ft (340m)
Codden Hill	42	Village hall, Landkey	SS 597310	5¾ miles (9km)	3 hrs	820ft (250m)
Dolton, Huish & the River Torridge	77	Dolton	SS 570121	8¾ miles (14.1km)	4½ hrs	1,380ft (420m)
Fremington Quay	12	Fremington Quay	SS 517334	3 miles (4.8km)	1½ hrs	n/a
Grand Western Canal	16	Manley Bridge	SS 986121	3¾ miles (6.1km)	1½ hrs	n/a
Great Torrington	18	Great Torrington	SS 494189	3¼ miles (5.2km)	2 hrs	375ft (115m)
Hartland Point & Speke's Mill Mouth	85	Rocket House, Hartland Quay	SS 226247	10½ miles (16.6km)	6 hrs	2,230ft (680m)
Hatherleigh & the River Lew	24	Hatherleigh	SS 540043	4½ miles (7.1km)	2½ hrs	345ft (105m)
Lundy Island	74	Marisco Tavern	SS 137440	8 miles (12.5km)	4 hrs	1,310ft (400m)
Malmsmead Hill & Badgworthy Water	22	Malmsmead	SS 791478	4 miles (6.4km)	2 hrs	655ft (200m)
Molland church & Common	33	Molland	SS 807283	5 miles (8km)	3 hrs	1,100ft (335m)
Morte Point	68	Mortehoe	SS 457452	7½ miles (12km)	4 hrs	1,885ft (575m)
Roadford Lake & Germansweek	27	Southweek Cross, Germansweek	SX 436929	5¼ miles (8.3km)	2½ hrs	540ft (165m)
Sandford, Shobrooke & Upton Hellions	81	Sandford	SS 830025	11½ miles (18.3km)	5½ hrs	1,395ft (425m)
Sheepwash & Buckland Filleigh	45	Sheepwash	SS 486063	6¼ miles (10.1km)	3 hrs	525ft (160m)
Tetcott	39	Lana	SX 339963	5½ miles (8.9km)	3 hrs	475ft (145m)
Trentishoe Down & Heddon's Mouth Cleave	62	Heddon's Gate	SS 655481	6¾ miles (10.8km)	4 hrs	1,490ft (455m)
Valley of Rocks	20	Valley of Rocks	SS 707497	3¾ miles (6km)	2 hrs	835ft (255m)
Watersmeet & the Foreland	89	Hillsford Bridge	SS 740477	10½ miles (16.6km)	6 hrs	2,835ft (865m)
Woody Bay & the Beacon	48	Woody Bay	SS 675486	5¾ miles (9km)	3½ hrs	1,410ft (430m)

Comments

An undulating exploration of Arlington Court's quiet parkland and beechwoods in the valley of the River Yeo, with an optional visit to Loxhore's 15th-century church.
A network of green lanes leads to an exhilarating route around the headlands flanking beautiful Croyde Bay, with a trudge along the wide sandy beach.
Rolling fields and tracks lead from Saxon Bampton to the unusual church at Morebath, with a return past the tree-covered Norman motte-and-bailey castle.
A hilly walk from one of North Devon's prettiest villages through fields and woods to the coast at Hele, followed by a lovely stretch of Coast Path to Water Mouth.
Level and peaceful water meadows in the Exe Valley: perfect for a gentle stroll on a summer's afternoon.
A level walk around an ancient landscape: a World Heritage Biosphere Reserve and the Great Field, worked since medieval times, overlooking the Taw–Torridge Estuary.
Clovelly without the crowds, along woodland tracks and through fields, with a return along the Coast Path via bluebell woods above Blackchurch Rock.
A lengthy walk along green lanes and across fields to the old seafaring hamlet of Buck's Mills, then pretty oak woodland to Peppercombe, site of an Iron Age hillfort.
A thorough exploration of rolling farmland and the wooded valleys of Little Dart and Taw in the heart of Devon, based on the old coaching town of Chulmleigh.
Expansive views across the Taw–Torridge Estuary and the North Devon coast can be enjoyed from the top of little-walked Codden Hill, 620ft above the Taw Valley.
You'll most likely be alone on this lengthy and hilly delve into remote countryside between Dolton and Merton above the River Torridge: a real step back in time.
Once a busy port and important industrial centre, the Quay and old railway line today provide easy walking opportunities – and a chance to spot birds on Fremington Pill.
An easy-to-follow level route along the old Tiverton branch line, with a return via the banks of the reed-fringed canal, closed to commercial traffic in the 1920s.
You'll discover history at every turn on this short yet hilly walk around 'the Cavalier town', perched on a bluff high above a bend of the great Torridge river.
A spectacular and tough route along the most magnificent (and hardest) section of the South West Coast Path: worth every ounce of effort!
The heart of Ruby Country: little-walked fields and tracks through gently rolling countryside around this market town, and a return along the tranquil River Lew.
Although the walk suggested can be completed on a day trip to Lundy Island, you'll be tempted to return for more – you have been warned!
One of the prettiest valleys on Exmoor is best experienced via this lovely route over Malmsmead Hill, with far-reaching views into the heart of the moor.
This remote village, nestled in hilly country in the shadow of one of Exmoor's quietest commons, is home to one of the most unspoilt Georgian churches in Devon.
An understandably popular section of the Coast Path, with a number of ascents and descents and glorious views across sandy coves en route to craggy Morte Point.
A walk along quiet tracks and fields with views across Roadford Lake, formed when the Wolf Valley was flooded in 1989, now popular with birdwatchers.
Mid Devon 'proper': rolling red-earthed fields, wooded valleys, quiet hamlets, ancient churches (and good pubs) are encountered on this long walk.
Pretty Sheepwash is the starting point for this route across fields and woods to Buckland Filleigh, with a return along lanes enjoying stunning views of Dartmoor.
Historic interest near the Cornish border: a medieval manor house and 13th-century church provide the focus for this walk through remote fields and woodlands above the Tamar Valley.
A hard climb from popular Heddon's Gate over Trentishoe Down is rewarded with a magical section of Coast Path and a steep descent under sessile oak woodland.
The strange sandstone formations are best viewed from the top of Southcliffe on this short yet tough route that climbs high above the valley, with wonderful coastal views.
A wonderful leg-stretcher: lengthy ascents and descents around the valleys of the East Lyn River and Hoar Oak Water, and stunning views from the Coast Path around The Foreland.
A surprisingly easy Exmoor coastal walk, utilising a Victorian carriage drive that runs above the Coast Path, with a chance for a halfway break at Heddon's Gate.

Introduction to North Devon

The predominantly rural county of Devon – the third largest in England – presents a wonderful range of walking opportunities to suit all tastes and abilities, and by combining the North Devon coast and Devon's Heartland in one book an extraordinary variety of landscapes can be explored.

The attractions of the South West Coast Path are undisputed, ranging from Exmoor's rolling hog's-back cliffs and high coastal hills *(Walk 20)* and one of Europe's most important dune systems *(Walk 9)* to the unforgiving switchback cliffs of the Hartland Peninsula, a mass of vertical tiltings and contortions caused by lateral pressure on the earth's crust 300 million years ago *(Walk 27).* These routes are undeniably popular, although rarely crowded compared, say, to parts of the Coast Path in South Devon.

Moving south into Devon's little-visited rural Heartland is a different matter altogether: a rolling landscape crisscrossed by a complex network of narrow hedged lanes, scattered farms and hamlets, remote churches, and a patchwork of small fields and pockets of woodland. In this relatively little-walked part of the county a circular route will often, by necessity, include stretches along quiet lanes, but these – often with stunning views south to Dartmoor – are a delight in themselves. It may take you a while (and some good map reading) to get to the start point; you may encounter poor waymarking, gates that are hard to open, field-edge detours, uneven and muddy ground. But on the plus side you will experience 'real' rural Devon, far off the beaten track and untouched by the effects of tourism – you may spot buzzards, red deer, and otters – and will be unlikely to meet anyone else on the route. Henry Williamson, author of the famous novel *Tarka the Otter* (published in 1927), christened this part of Devon 'The Country of the Two Rivers' and summed up its qualities thus 'the country covered by webbed paw, fin, clawed pad and pinion' – and in parts of Devon's Heartland little has changed since he penned those words. Those 'two rivers' are the great Taw and the Torridge that wend their way through pastoral and wooded landscapes to their confluence just north of Appledore on the north coast *(Walks 4, 9, 14 and 25).*

One point that must be made is that Devon is a hilly county. Not on the scale of Cumbria, of course (although stretches of the South West Coast Path frequently catch out those who have little idea of how tough on both knees and lungs its steep ascents and descents can be); but those unused to such exertions and who prefer to keep on the flat would do better visiting, for example, the Somerset Levels. That said, the walks in this book are graded according to length and degree of difficulty, and there are some easy routes which utilise river estuary paths and disused railways. *Walks 1, 2, 3 and 9* can be described as having a negligible height gain.

The limekiln at Heddon's Mouth

Several of the routes make use of the area's extensive network of green lanes, unmetalled hedged ways that date from the time when the majority of the population lived in the countryside, linking farms, villages and remote cottages. Today these provide wonderful traffic-free walking routes: especially good examples are followed on the inland stretch of *Walk 27* on the Hartland peninsula.

Facilities

When it comes to facilities, those routes nearer centres of population will be better served. But an encouraging sign in these days of post office and village shop closures, and poor rural public transport services, is the number of community shops encountered in tucked-away villages – Sheepwash *(Walk 14)*, Berrynarbor *(Walk 17)* and Sandford *(Walk 26)*, for example – where villagers have worked together to keep the shop going (or, in some cases, to start a new one), relying largely on volunteer labour. And the same goes for pubs: in North Devon, an area popular with holidaymakers, you will come across a good number of thriving pubs. But pubs in Devon's less popular Heartland, way off the tourist trail, are fighting their corner too. Pubs in more remote villages have to rely on local all-year-round trade, and very often excellent locally sourced food (and more reasonable prices) will be found in such establishments. Note that away from the more tourist-oriented areas food is rarely served all day: best to carry your own if you are likely to miss opening hours.

Waymarking

The majority of walks in this book stick to foot and bridlepaths that are clearly marked on the OS map. However, when walking on open access moorland (such as Exmoor) you will find that rights of way marked on the map do not always match what is on the ground: Malmsmead Hill and Molland Common *(Walks 6*

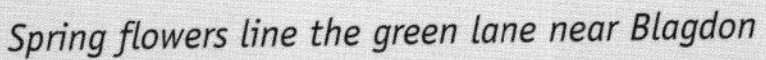

Spring flowers line the green lane near Blagdon

nd 10), for example, are threaded with a network of indistinct paths and it is asy to go wrong. Follow directions carefully and keep a close eye on the map: nd if you go wrong backtrack to your last known position and have another o. Be aware too that some infrequently walked paths in Mid Devon tend to be ess well maintained and hence signage is not as reliable.

esignated routes

number of 'official' routes cross the area, and many of the walks make use of dd stretches of these. Some – the South West Coast Path, for example – are vell waymarked and the route easy to follow; others – such as the Little Dart idge and Valley – are barely marked on the ground.

North Devon's stretch of the South West Coast Path, which runs from Minehead in Somerset to the shores of Poole Harbour in Dorset, is one of the est along its 630-mile (1,014km) length. Devon is lucky to hold two-thirds of xmoor's 34-mile (55km) coastline, whereas only one-third of the total land rea of the National Park falls within the county.

The Two Moors way runs for 102 miles (164km) right across Devon's Ieartland, linking Dartmoor with the north coast at Lynmouth. The section etween the two moors traverses unspoilt countryside, and the route links with he Little Dart and Valley Walk at Witheridge, which runs west through ecluded pastoral and woodland landscapes for 11 miles (17.7km) to the Taw Valley, with a spur to Chulmleigh *(Walk 21).* Farther east is the Exe Valley Way, almost 50 miles (80km) from its source on Exmoor to its mouth on the south coast, passing through Bampton *(Walk 11),* Tiverton (with a link to the Grand Western Canal, *Walk 3*) and Brampford Speke *(Walk 2).* To the south the 43-mile (69km) Devonshire Heartland Way through Devon's traditional 'redlands' (New Red Sandstones, laid down in the Permian period c 280–200 million years ago) links with the Exe Valley Way, and crosses both the Two Moors Way and Tarka Trail *(Walk 26).* Around Hatherleigh and Holsworthy – truly 'undiscovered' Devon! – is a series of waymarked Ruby Trails intended to further understanding of this area, little visited even by those living within the county *(Walks 7, 12 and 14).* And cropping up all over the place you will find the Tarka Trail, named after the hero of Henry Williamson's novel, an 180-mile (297km) figure-of-eight route centred on Barnstaple and one of the country's longest continuous traffic-free walking and cycling paths. Some 30 miles (48km) are constructed on the routes of the old railway lines of North Devon providing the opportunity for easy level walks *(Walk 1).*

This book includes a list of waypoints alongside the description of the walk, so that you can enjoy the full benefits of gps should you wish to. For more information on using your gps, read the *Pathfinder® Guide GPS for Walkers,* by gps teacher and navigation trainer, Clive Thomas (ISBN 978-0-7117-4445-5). For essential information on map reading and basic navigation, read the *Pathfinder® Guide Map Reading Skills* by outdoor writer, Terry Marsh (ISBN 978-0-7117-4978-8). Both titles are available in bookshops or can be ordered online at www.totalwalking.co.uk

Fremington Quay

Start	Fremington Quay
Distance	3 miles (4.8km)
Height gain	Negligible
Approximate time	1½ hours
Parking	Designated parking area (free) at Fremington Quay, signed off B3233 at Fremington, 2½ miles west of Barnstaple
Route terrain	Level tracks and field paths
Ordnance Survey maps	Landranger 180 (Barnstaple & Ilfracombe), Explorer 139 (Bideford, Ilfracombe & Barnstaple)

GPS waypoints

- SS 517 334
- A SS 517 340
- B SS 520 335
- C SS 527 334
- D SS 522 329
- E SS 520 326

Fremington Quay, once the busiest port between Bristol and Land's End, dates from the 1840s when silting of the Taw Estuary prevented large vessels from reaching Barnstaple. Today the line of the old North Devon Railway carries cyclists and walkers through this delightful spot. This easy walk follows the Tarka Trail along the Taw before returning along tranquil Fremington Pill.

From the end of the parking area pick up a small path under trees (just left of the drive to Railway Cottage) onto the foreshore. Walk along the foreshore to reach an abandoned limekiln on the right. The Taw Vale Railway & Dock Company was formed in 1838 to build a deep-water quay at Fremington, and a horse-drawn line to Barnstaple was constructed. In 1854, when the main North Devon Railway line reached Barnstaple, and the line to Bideford via Fremington further developed the following year, the Quay's fortunes received another boost. Lime and coal were landed here from South Wales (and vast amounts of ball clay from Merton and Petersmarland in Mid Devon exported) and burned locally to produce fertiliser to aid local farmers. William Thorne, a local industrialist, was chairman of the company: his house, built in 1872, now houses the Barnstaple & North Devon Museum.

Just past the limekiln turn right A on a hedged track, which soon bears right, and eventually reaches a bridge over the Tarka Trail. Do not cross the bridge, but bear right B down steps onto the Trail. Turn left under the bridge (watch out for bikes) and continue along the old railway line through a long cutting – look out for blue field scabious and meadow brown butterflies in summer – eventually to emerge into open country with extensive saltmarsh and mudflats leading to the River Taw on the left (the Taw Estuary provides important habitats for a wide range of specialised plants and wildlife, and is a huge wintering ground for migrant birds). In summer look out for sea lavender and

a aster (one of the
w plants that can
pe with immersion
seawater, and
hich helps stabilise
e marshes).

After just under
: mile look for a
otpath sign right,
nd turn right C
own steps to cross a
ile and boardwalk.
Valk up a gently
scending hedged
rassy track to meet
nother at Clampitt;
ırn right. The track
oon bears sharp left
o meet a lane on a
orner, opposite a thatched cottage.
'urn right; about 75 yds later turn left
D on a public footpath on a grassy
ath (damp underfoot after rain) to
merge into a field. Follow the left edge
o pass through a hedge gap and
ontinue in the same direction: the
vaters of Fremington Pill – once
navigable to its head at Muddlebridge
(before the building of Fremington
Quay a local port operated from the Pill)
– come into view ahead. At the field end
drop to cross a stile onto a lane.

Turn right E and follow the narrow
lane back along the Pill towards the
quay (it can be busy at peak times, but
drivers are warned of walkers' presence
and limited to 15mph). The lane bears
sharp right; just before meeting houses
(right) turn left at the edge of a small
parking area on a concrete path that
leads to the Tarka Trail, and turn right.
About 25 yds later turn left to walk
along the edge of the quay, eventually
turning left at the end to the car park.
The railway closed in the 1960s, and the
last ship to visit Fremington was the
Dutch merchant vessel *Dec* in 1969.

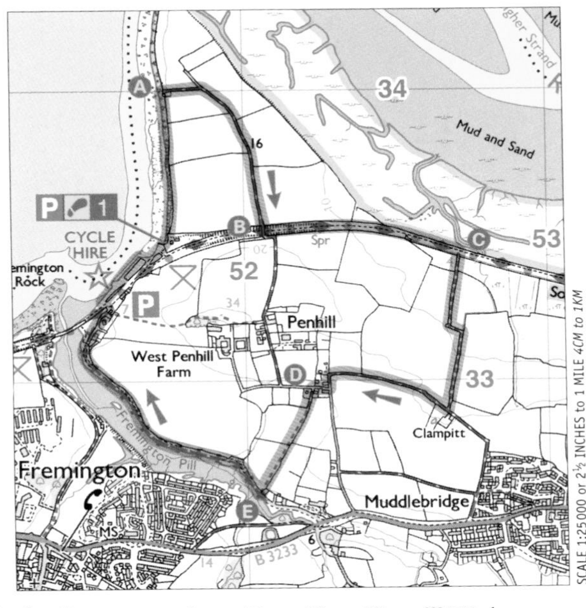

Although all but the old station and signal box have been demolished (now housing a Heritage Centre and **café**) you can still see the outline of the platform, and the depth of the waters off the quay. From the 17th to 19th centuries Fremington was also known for the Fremington Pottery, based on the discovery locally of a seam of plastic fine-grained clay. Functional pots, and a few decorative pieces, were exported from Fremington to Wales, Ireland, France and the New World.

The Tarka Trail crosses Fremington Pill on the old railway bridge

Brampford Speke & the River Exe

Start	Brampford Speke
Distance	3 miles (4.8km) + optional 2-mile (3.2km) extension
Height gain	Negligible
Approximate time	1½ hours (1 hour for extension)
Parking	Laneside parking near the church in Brampford Speke (note Church Drive is private), 4 miles north of Exeter off the A377
Route terrain	Level fields, tracks, country lanes
Ordnance Survey maps	Landranger 192 (Exeter & Sidmouth), Explorer 114 (Exeter & the Exe Valley)

GPS waypoints

- Start SX 926 982
- A SX 927 985
- B SX 936 980
- C SX 939 991
- D SX 935 991
- E SX 926 984
- F SX 918 982
- G SX 913 978

The floodplain of the Exe, where the river meanders through beautiful water meadows near the cob-and-thatch village of Brampford Speke, is delightful. An optional extension runs through fields and water meadows to the west of the village.

The walk begins at Church Drive.

Start: Walk towards St Peter's Church, turning left through the churchyard on the Devonshire Heartland Way/Exe Valley Way. Pass round the west end and through a gate onto a path. Follow this, passing through a kissing-gate en route, to reach a lane via an arch and gate.

Turn right; drop steeply to cross the River Exe via a footbridge, to a footpath junction. Turn right A; two grassy paths cross the meadow ahead. The right of way follows the wire fence (left fork), soon crossing a bridge, before joining the other path. A kissing-gate leads onto the disused railway embankment. Emerge from the trees – look right across the river to the church above a low sandstone cliff. Pass through a kissing-gate, and follow the embankment along the left edge of the field. Pass through a gate and cross a bridge; keep ahead on a broad fenced path towards Stoke Canon. Where the embankment bears away right keep slightly left through a kissing-gate, then along the right edge of the next field. Pass through a kissing-gate onto a fenced path to reach a lane via a gate by the level crossing on the Exeter–Paddington line.

Turn left B; follow the quiet lane through pretty countryside for ¾ mile to reach medieval Burrow Cross.

Turn left C; past cottages the lane reduces to a hedged track. Where this bears sharp right turn left D, almost immediately passing through a kissing-gate onto a track, which bears left on meeting the river. Continue along the left bank, soon crossing a stile. Follow the river to pass through a double kissing-gate. About 50 yds later the riverbank bears away right; keep ahead, aiming for the far left corner of the field, soon meeting a hedge left; pass through a metal gate (open) at the field end. Follow the left edge of the next to pass through a kissing-gate under trees. Keep ahead briefly then bear left towards the footbridge A. Cross over and ascend to the arch; turn left to return to your car.

The walk can be extended from this point. From the arch turn right; within a few steps bear left at the junction to a T-junction of lanes.

Turn left (primary school left), and after 75 yds turn right E on Sandy Way. Pass houses, and negotiate two left/right kinks; where the lane soon bears sharp right keep ahead F through a gate. Bear left across the field corner and follow the left edge. The path bears left into woodland, crosses a stile/ boardwalk (boggy in winter) to meet a stream, then crosses a double-railed footbridge/boardwalk. Keep ahead; emerge from trees, and follow the left edge of the field. Where the hedge bears 90 degrees left the footpath bears half right into the field, then bears left and straightens, aiming for a footpath post by a hedge gap. Follow the left edge of the next field towards houses in Upton Pyne. The path passes Cox's Hill Farm to reach a T-junction.

Turn left G; the rough hedged track eventually enters fields. Keep along the right edge of the first and second, dropping gently. Look out for a small gate right, and pass through: cross a footbridge and go through another gate. Continue across water meadows, soon crossing another footbridge; keep along the left edge (boggy in winter) to cross another. Now ascend slightly to pass through a kissing-gate; eventually the path bears left between hedges to reach another. Follow the left edge of the next field towards Brampford Speke. You will see a kissing-gate and narrow hedged path leading to the lane.

Turn left for your car.

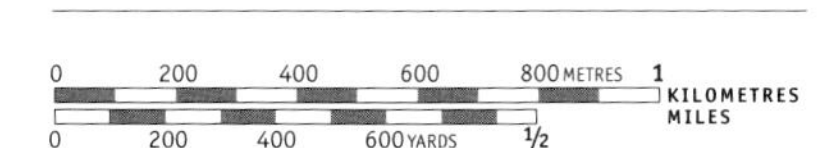

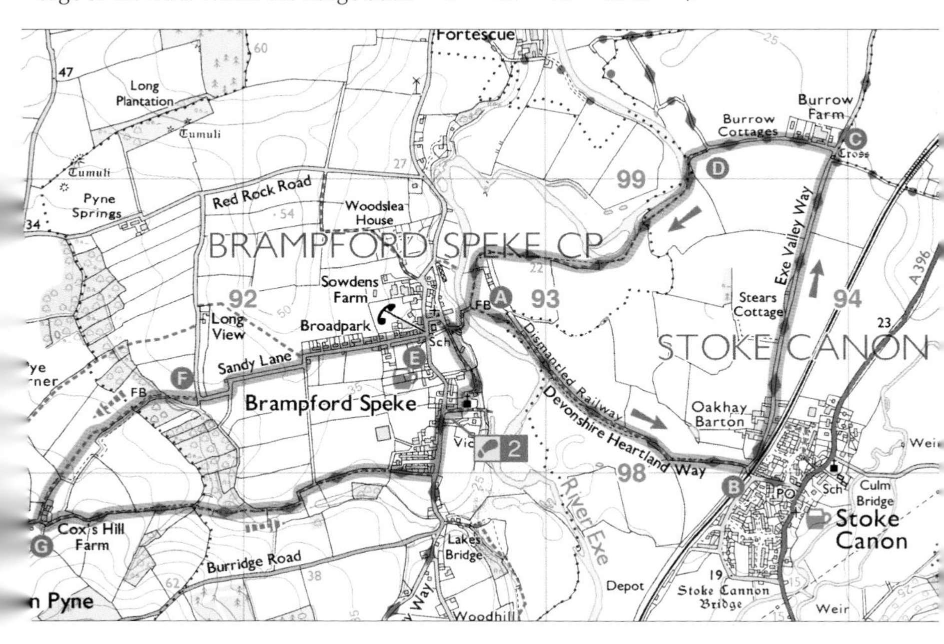

Grand Western Canal

Start	Manley Bridge
Distance	3¾ miles (6.1km)
Height gain	Negligible
Approximate time	1½ hours
Parking	Parking area (free) at Manley Bridge signed off the Halberton road 1 mile east of Tiverton
Route terrain	Level track (old railway), lanes, canal towpath
Ordnance Survey maps	Landranger 181 (Minehead & Brendon Hills), Explorer 114 (Exeter & the Exe Valley)

GPS waypoints

- SS 986 121
- Ⓐ SS 987 123
- Ⓑ SS 965 127
- Ⓒ SS 964 126
- Ⓓ SS 963 124

A level walk that's packed with historic interest, following the line of the Tiverton branch line of the Bristol & Exeter Railway, dating from 1847, and returning along the canal, part of a grand scheme to link the Bristol and English channels; only the Tiverton–Taunton section was ever completed. Look out for herons, moorhens, dragonflies, waterlilies ... and cyclists.

If the parking area is full there are wide verges on the approach road from the Tiverton–Halberton road.

Walk away from the canal along Manley Lane. Cross a bridge and turn immediately left Ⓐ to descend onto the disused railway track; the railway closed to passenger traffic in 1964. This part of the route is shared with Sustrans National Cycle Route 3 – Land's End to Bristol – and is also popular with local cyclists, so keep a look out. Follow this through a cutting, then under Black Bridge into open country. Pass under another bridge, after which houses are reached on the edge of Tiverton. The path becomes tarmac and has a more urban feel as it passes under substantial Tidcombe Lane Bridge. The old line ends at a gate, with a busy road and roundabout ahead Ⓑ; the town centre is signed left.

Bear left to meet a road; turn right along the pavement. At the end of a parking area (right) turn left up Lewis Avenue Ⓒ. At the top cross Harrowby Close and continue ahead, uphill, through houses. The high wall at the edge of the Canal Basin (and holding the limekilns, in use until at least 1895) rises ahead. The road narrows and continues left; bear right off it on a narrow

Barge on the Grand Western Canal

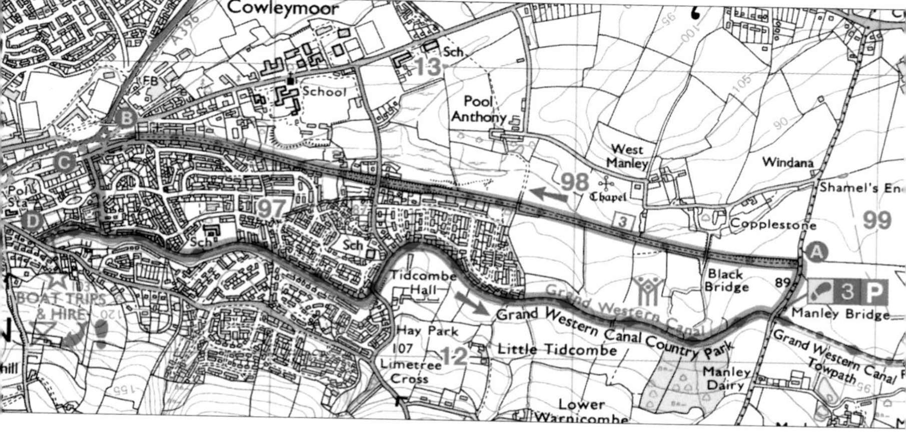

unmarked path past a metal post and keep ahead to reach the end of the Basin parking area with 16th-century thatched (Lime Kiln Cottage) **Canal Tea Room** and Garden left (the only thatched building left in Tiverton). Turn left to ascend to the canal, then right for the Basin, Visitor Centre Ⓓ and **Duck's Ditty Café Bar** (licensed), picnic tables, boats and great views over Tiverton and the rolling Mid Devon countryside. The 11-mile section of canal between Tiverton and Lowdwells was built between 1810 and 1814, largely for the transport of limestone from quarries at Westleigh. Tons of limestone were burned here to supply farmers with fertiliser to lessen the acidity of Mid Devon's culm soils: some came from as far as 30 miles away to collect it by horse and cart. Competition from the railways forced the closure of the canal, although limestone was transported here until 1924.

To return follow the towpath along the left bank of the canal, soon leaving the Basin behind. Look out for an old stone pier on the opposite bank: the grooves for a stop-gate are still visible. This would have been used to seal off part of the canal when repairs were needed to this section. Pass under a footbridge; the canal bears left to pass

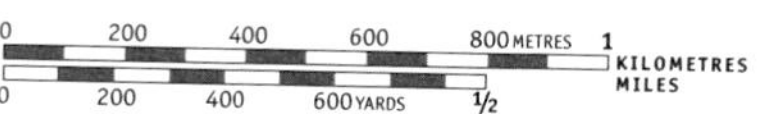

under Tidcombe Bridge (the canal loops north here due to the Bishop of Exeter's refusal to allow it to run within 100 yds of his home at Tidcombe Hall!), after which fields appear on the far bank and there's a more rural feel. You may see a brightly painted horse-drawn barge drifting along the waters: trips are run from the basin from spring to autumn. Note a milestone (Milestone I, indicating it's a mile from the canal basin) by the path. The towpath widens, with lovely rural views, and passes under Warnicombe Bridge. Just before Manley Bridge note a memorial by the towpath to two pilots whose plane crashed here in 1961; parts of their plane were dredged up in 2003, and the memorial placed here on the 45th anniversary of the event.

Pass under Manley Bridge, and turn left for the car park. If you want to extend your walk a little continue along the canal to reach the aqueduct over the old railway line. In places you will see swathes of waterlilies in summer, harvested until the mid 1960s from a horse-drawn boat, and sent around the country to be used in funeral wreaths.

Great Torrington

Start	Great Torrington
Distance	3¼ miles (5.2km)
Height gain	375 feet (115m)
Approximate time	2 hours
Parking	Castle Hill car park; Great Torrington is on the A386, 7 miles south of Bideford
Route terrain	Riverside woodland tracks and meadows, well-surfaced paths through commons; one steep descent and one lengthy yet gradual ascent
Ordnance Survey maps	Landranger 180 (Barnstaple & Ilfracombe), Explorer 126 (Clovelly & Hartland)

GPS waypoints

- SS 494 189 (start)
- Ⓐ SS 498 188
- Ⓑ SS 499 188
- Ⓒ SS 498 187
- Ⓓ SS 488 187
- Ⓔ SS 480 196

Known as the 'Cavalier town' – the Battle of Torrington in 1646 marked the end of Royalist resistance in the Westcountry during the English Civil War – Great Torrington provides the opportunity for a delightful walk.

From the car park look over the Torridge Valley. Note two long, thin fields – strips or 'straps' – rare examples of a medieval field system and once part of seven 'Leper Fields', cultivated by inmates from the leper hospital 'safely' sited over the river in Taddiport (see later).

The walk starts from the far left corner of the car park, by a section of castle wall (the site's history is patchy: it is known that Norman fortifications were destroyed in 1228, and that Richard de Merton built a castle and keep here in the 14th century). Pass through an arch; turn left on a tarmac path past castellated walls built by John, Lord Rolle in the mid 19th century. Pass a picnic area, with wonderful views towards Taddiport.

The path (George's Path) descends gently, with views towards the Town Mills (also built by Lord Rolle) at New Bridge, with RHS Rosemoor Gardens beyond. On meeting a grassy area turn sharp right Ⓐ downhill and descend to a pointed stone monument, built in June 1818 to commemorate the Battle of Waterloo.

From the monument turn left and continue downhill on a narrow path (Monument Path). It bears right towards the A386; before meeting the road turn right Ⓑ down steps (Lady Wash), and descend to reach a T-junction on the banks of the Torridge. Turn right Ⓒ and walk along the former Rolle Canal (opened to traffic in 1827; parts were sold off in 1871 to make way for the London & South West Railway) – this section was later filled in and became a toll road, and now provides a peaceful, level walking route. Where you see steps dropping left to the river you have a choice, either between the old toll road or taking the uneven and narrow path near the water's edge, which eventually rejoins the toll road up steps.

Chantry Chapel, Taddiport

At that point turn left round a wooden barrier and keep ahead, then bear right along the edge of riverside meadows (Ladies Island) to eventually cross a stile onto the road **D** at Taddiport Bridge, once the site of Taddiport Quay from where oak bark (for tanning) and ball clay from Petersmarland were exported (**Torridge Inn** right).

For a short detour turn left over the bridge to find (right) the atmospheric Chantry Chapel of the Leper Hospital of St Mary Magdalene, first identified in 1310.

Recross the bridge; turn left on the riverside path to pass the disused milk factory. Cross a stile by a weir and walk through an area of rough grassland before returning to riverside meadows. Cross another stile and continue along the left edge of a large field. Cross a stile and pass the sewage works. An area of light woodland leads to steps onto the old toll road. Turn left; just before reaching the old railway bridge (now carrying the Tarka Trail – for the **Puffing Billy** pub keep straight ahead) turn right **E** up steps. Turn right at the top; climb steeply to meet a T-junction; turn right on a tarmac path. Follow this, climbing gradually, across Great Torrington Common (the Commons cover 365 acres and were given to the town in the 12th century) to meet a road on Limers Hill.

Cross over; at the fork keep left along the top of the common with views of the chapel at Taddiport. The path joins a road; bear right along it. Where it bears away right downhill keep ahead through Rack Park (where woven cloth was once stretched and bleached by the sun). Meet Mill Street (down which defeated Royalist troops fled en route for Cornwall) and keep ahead; on meeting South Street keep ahead to find the car park (right). The Torrington 1646 exhibition (in the car park) will provide you with information on Torrington's role during the Civil War. ●

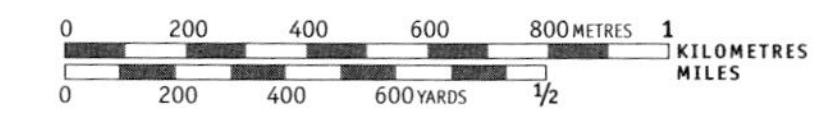

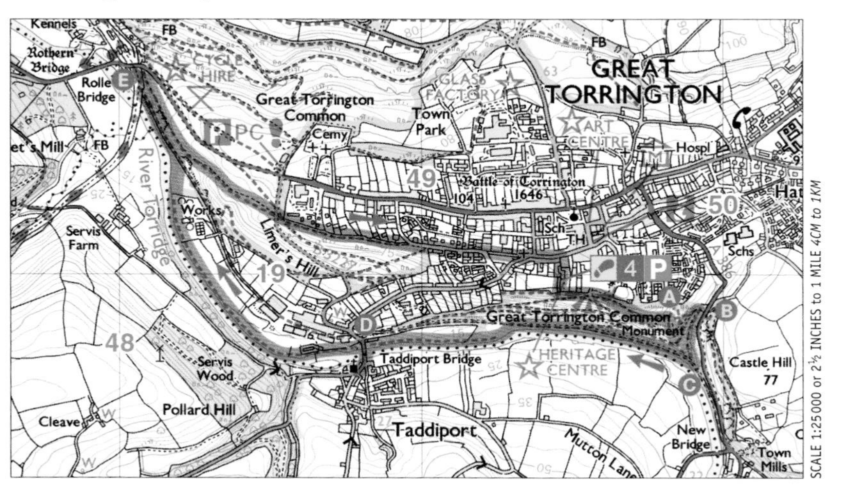

SCALE 1:25 000 or 2½ INCHES to 1 MILE 4CM to 1KM

The Valley of Rocks

Start	The Valley of Rocks
Distance	3¾ miles (6km)
Height gain	835 feet (255m)
Approximate time	2 hours
Parking	Car park (fee paying) in Valley of Rocks; signed from Lynton, 1½ miles from A39 at Barbrook
Route terrain	Woodland tracks, rough pasture, one long steep ascent/descent
Dog friendly	To be kept on leads (goats)
Ordnance Survey maps	Landranger 180 (Barnstaple & Ilfracombe), Explorer OL9 (Exmoor)

GPS waypoints

- SS 707 497
- A SS 712 492
- B SS 701 492
- C SS 696 489
- D SS 705 496
- E SS 710 499

Most visitors to the Valley of Rocks choose the easy options of wandering through the valley bottom or along the tarmac North Walk from Lynton. This short yet lofty route escapes the crowds by climbing high above the valley, with spectacular views over its craggy rock formations and lovely Lee Bay, one of only two sandy beaches on the Exmoor coast.

From the car park turn left up the road past **Mother Meldrum's Tea Room** – Mother Meldrum featured in R.D. Blackmore's *Lorna Doone (see Walk 6)*, and is thought to be based on Aggie Norman, a witch who lived in the Valley of Rocks in the 19th century. Towards the end of the cricket pitch bear right on a grassy path signed to Lynton that runs behind another car park/picnic area and through a kissing-gate. Continue through woodland, rising gently. Meet a footpath junction at the start of a walled section and turn sharp right A, still climbing, signed Lee Abbey over Southcliffe.

Despite ascending around 230ft in a short distance, height is gained surprisingly easily. Initially there are views right to Hollerday Hill: Chimney Rock, to its left, is where 18th-century wreckers set lights to lure unsuspecting ships onto the rocks below. The path narrows and continues to climb to emerge from the trees with amazing views over the valley and coast. It is thought that the Valley of Rocks – a dry valley – was formed by the cutting off of either one or both of the Lyn rivers during the Ice Age, and the subsequent changing of its course; freeze–thaw action has resulted in the extraordinary sandstone tors that are dotted about the valley, and screes of weathered material. Continue to climb to pass through a kissing-gate into open country; keep ahead along a hedgebank, bearing sharp left. The biggest tor on the opposite side of the valley (at the left end) is Castle Rock, with Rugged Jack – said to be named after the leader of a group of revellers turned to stone

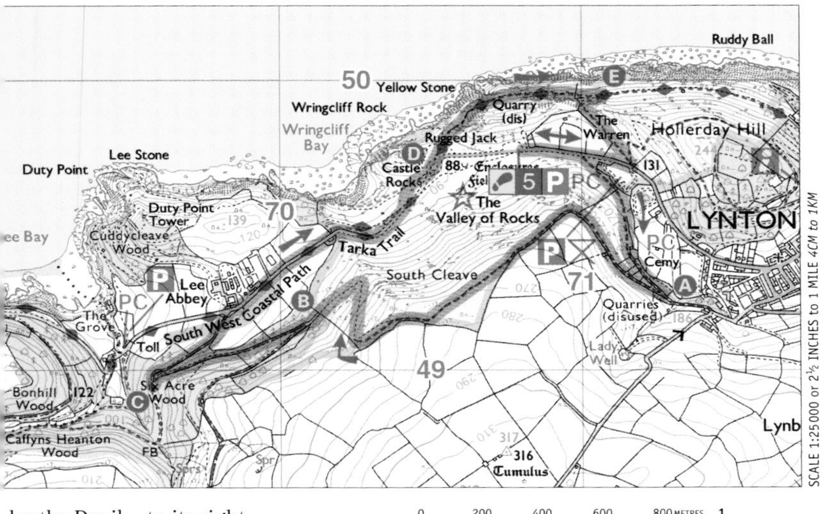

by the Devil – to its right.

Continue along the hedgebank *(note there is a very steep drop on the right)*. Look out for goats (you can often smell them before you see them!): wild Cheviot goats were introduced in 1976 to replace the feral goats that had been here for centuries, and are occasionally culled when their numbers get too high. Where the wall bears away left follow the path as it bears right along the top of the hill, eventually to meet a wall and gate ahead. Bear right downhill on a narrow path, heading for Lee Bay; note Duty Point Tower, a mid 19th-century folly, on Duty Point and sprawling buildings associated with Lee Abbey, a Christian conference and residential centre since 1946. Much of the estate is a designated SSSI on account of its rich and diverse flora and fauna. The site – which has never accommodated an abbey – was originally owned by Christian monks from Forde Abbey in Dorset; the current building dates from the mid 19th century. Descend steeply, eventually bearing sharp right along the contours; on meeting a big rock turn sharp left towards Six Acre Wood, to meet a gate **B**.

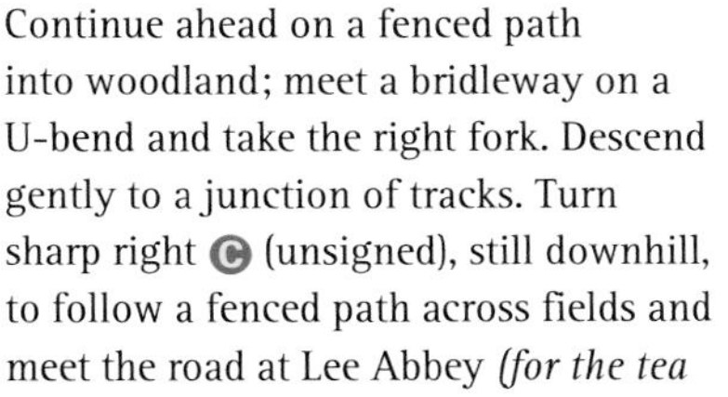

Continue ahead on a fenced path into woodland; meet a bridleway on a U-bend and take the right fork. Descend gently to a junction of tracks. Turn sharp right **C** (unsigned), still downhill, to follow a fenced path across fields and meet the road at Lee Abbey *(for the tea cottage at Lee Bay, open Tuesday–Saturday and Bank Holiday Monday during the summer holidays, turn left downhill)*.

Turn right uphill, soon passing the lodge house. On drawing level with Castle Rock (left) look for a small grassy path bearing left off the road. Re-meet the road by a Coast Path sign; turn left **D**, signed Lynton, aiming for a tarmac path ahead that passes between Castle Rock and Rugged Jack (the North Walk to Lynton). Continue below rocky outcrops, eventually climbing to another junction; turn sharp right to leave the Coast Path **E**, signed Lynton and Hollerday Hill. Climb steeply uphill then descend gently past the cricket pitch. At the end of the wall turn right downhill to meet the road opposite the toilets. Turn right for the car park. ●

Malmsmead Hill & Badgworthy Water

Start	Malmsmead
Distance	4 miles (6.4km)
Height gain	655 feet (200m)
Approximate time	2 hours
Parking	Car park (fee paying); Malmsmead signed off A39 between Lynmouth and Porlock, 1 mile east of Countisbury
Route terrain	Lanes, moorland, wooded valley; rough underfoot at times; *do not attempt in misty conditions*
Dog friendly	To be kept on leads on Malmsmead Hill (stock)
Ordnance Survey maps	Landranger 180 (Barnstaple & Ilfracombe), Explorer OL9 (Exmoor)

GPS waypoints

Start	SS 791 478
A	SS 784 473
B	SS 781 469
C	SS 787 460
D	SS 792 457
E	SS 792 454

The beautiful valley of the Badgworthy Water is one of Exmoor's hotspots on account of the area featuring in R.D. Blackmore's famous novel Lorna Doone, *published in 1869. This short yet leg-stretching route has a steep start, then follows rough paths over Malmsmead Hill before descending to the riverside path just north of Lank Coombe, Blackmore's 'Doone Valley'.*

Leave the car park past the toilets and keep ahead to meet the lane on a corner. Cross over and walk up Post Lane for ½ mile, climbing steadily and steepening just before crossing a cattle-grid at Lower Ball Gate to reach the edge of Malmsmead Hill. The lane levels off a little: after 200 yds bear left on a bridlepath **A** to Dry Bridge and Badgworthy Valley, a broad grassy path which passes to the left of a telegraph pole. The path bears slightly right and drops into the top of a shallow combe (damp in winter), where you will see three rough paths: do not follow the bridleway which bears left but keep straight ahead on the right-hand path, which runs up the right side of the combe. Keep uphill across rough grassland, eventually bearing left to a stony track.

Turn left **B**; follow the track across Malmsmead Hill, enjoying virtually 360-degree views from the highest point (1,276ft): on a clear day South Wales is visible north across the Bristol Channel. Eventually the track bears sharp right: keep ahead through a gate in a bank **C** onto Great Black Hill, with views ahead to the wooded Badgworthy Valley and the swell of South Common beyond: you'll get a feeling of being out on Exmoor 'proper'. The broad, rough path bears half left and drops gently downhill across heather moorland (aim just to the right of a clump of conifers running up Land Combe on the other side of the valley).

The path becomes more distinct and bears slightly right to meet the top of Badgworthy Wood D; it narrows and steepens (rocky underfoot) and descends beneath beautiful oaks – sounds of rushing waters in the valley below – to meet another track. Turn left downhill to meet the riverside bridlepath in Badgworthy Combe. Lank Combe and Hoccombe Combe, the latter the site of a deserted medieval village, can be found by a short diversion right: a pleasant riverside walk into the heart of 'Doone Country'. Legend has it that the Doones – thought to be a notorious band of outlaws who settled on Exmoor in the days of the Monmouth Rebellion of 1685 – settled in Hoccombe Combe.

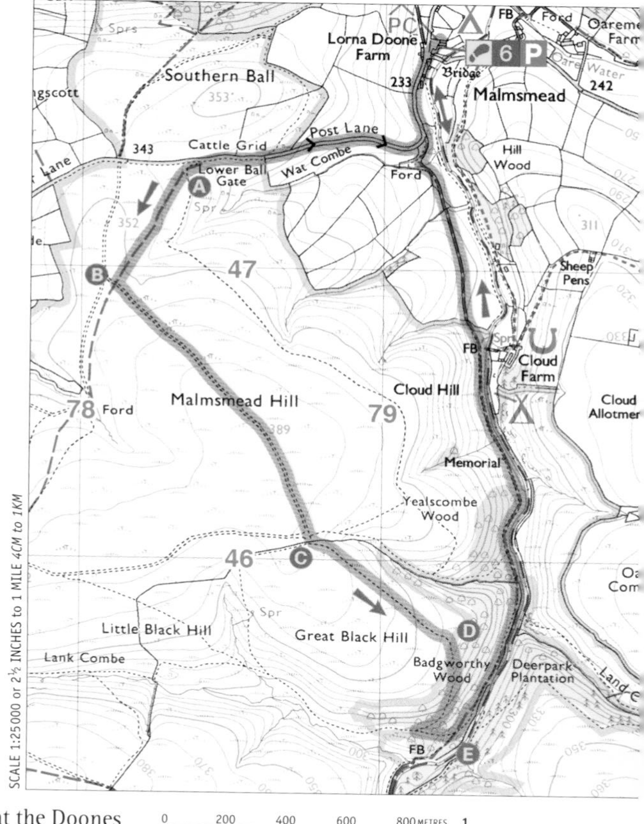

Turn left E along the bridlepath, which can be muddy in places after wet weather. Pass a permissive bridlepath across the river right and continue under pretty oaks, eventually passing through a gate into more open country, with Yealscombe Wood left. Eventually the track splits, so take the riverside path here (more even and drier), rejoining the bridlepath by the Blackmore memorial, erected by the Lorna Doone Centenary Committee. Reach a junction of paths with **Cloud Farm** (refreshments) across the river (footbridge). Keep ahead and climb away from the river to pass through a gate: continue along a banked track to pass through another gate. The track eventually bears left then right uphill to meet a gate onto Post Lane.

Bear right down the lane to return to Malmsmead. Before returning to your car turn right to take a look at 'Lorna Doone Farm' (dating from Saxon times), **The Buttery** (refreshments) and Malmsmead's pretty 17th-century packhorse bridge. The 1,000-year-old Church of St Mary's at Oare, where Lorna was shot on the day of her wedding to Jan Ridd, can be found about 3/4 mile farther along the lane. Blackmore's grandfather was rector of Oare parish from 1809 to 1842, and he would no doubt have had access to parish records and local legends to inspire his imagination.

Hatherleigh & the River Lew

Start	Hatherleigh
Distance	4½ miles (7.1km)
Height gain	345 feet (105m)
Approximate time	2½ hours
Parking	Car park (fee-paying) in Hatherleigh; off the A386 between Okehampton and Great Torrington
Route terrain	Unimproved grassland, tracks, quiet lanes
Dog friendly	Dogs to be kept on leads
Ordnance Survey maps	Landranger 191 (Okehampton & North Dartmoor), Explorer 113 (Okehampton)

GPS waypoints

Start	SS 540 043
A	SS 539 041
B	SS 529 045
C	SS 521 046
D	SS 516 054
E	SS 521 056
F	SS 531 052

Hatherleigh, in the heart of 'Ruby Country' – the name is taken from the Red Ruby Devon breed of cattle – is known throughout the county for its weekly livestock market, dating from a Charter of 1693. This walk starts from the famous 'Sheep' sculpture, and follows a gentle route through the surrounding farmland before returning along the pretty River Lew.

Walk towards Bridge Street and turn right. Cross the River Lew; on reaching the A386 cross to the right of the roundabout.

Turn right **A** on a tarmac driveway, passing the cricket club. Where the track bears away right, and the concrete way goes to houses left, cross a stile in between. Follow a track through the field, passing through a gate at the end; keep along the right edge of the next field. After about 200 yds bear right through a gate at a footpath fork and cross the next field diagonally, aiming for the far right corner (boggy in winter). Cross a double stile/footbridge; bear half right across the next field, aiming for an oak tree in the corner. Cross the stile and walk along a bank, dropping down steps. Bear right towards North Waterhouse Farm –

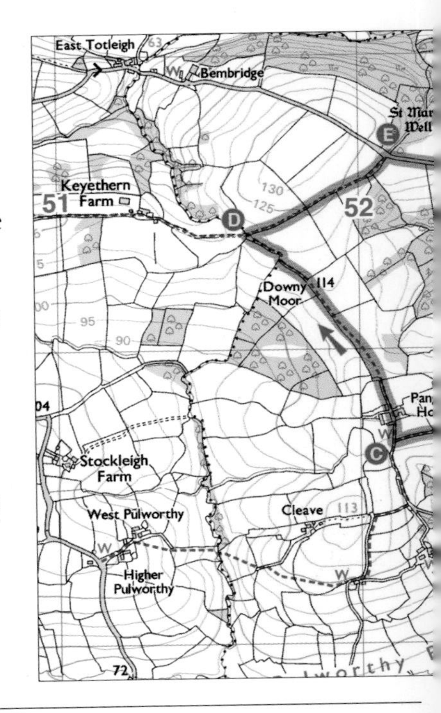

dating from 1500 – then bear left down a track to meet the embankment of the former Torrington to Halwill Junction railway line (1925 to 1965) Ⓑ.

Pass through the old railway gate (note the sign 'Penalty for not shutting gate £2'!) then cross Pulworthy Brook via pull-apart stiles and a footbridge. Cross the next field, bearing slightly left towards a gate. Go through and walk uphill, bearing slightly right, to another gate with a footpath arrow. Walk up the left edge of the next field. Bear left at the top through a gate; turn right and walk up the field, parallel to and eventually against the left hedge. At the top follow the hedge left to a footpath post; cross a stile into a field. Bear slightly right uphill, aiming for a small gate by a larger one. Go through and turn left (note the path on the OS map is marked to the south, not north, of the hedge); look left for views of Dartmoor.

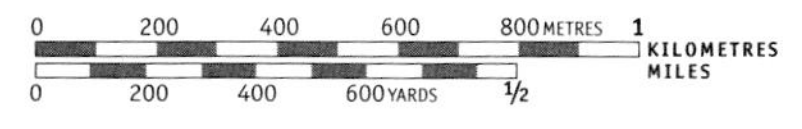

Pass through a gate to meet a track on a bend: keep ahead, passing below Pangkor House, to a T-junction.

Turn right Ⓒ; the track climbs gently past the house; pass through a gate onto a hedged path. Cross a footbridge/kissing-gate and walk up the left edge of the next field (damp underfoot). Cross a stile/footbridge/stile and take the same line up the next to meet a stand of willow (boggy ground) in the top corner. Cross a footbridge/stile onto a track, with deer fencing (Keyethern Farm) left.

Turn right Ⓓ; the track leads to a lane. Turn right Ⓔ, eventually dropping steeply to cross Lewer Bridge, dating from 1844; the Lew meets the Torridge just north of Hatherleigh. Immediately turn right Ⓕ and bear left across a meadow, eventually to cross the railway embankment via kissing-gates and steps. Follow the left bank of the river, at times climbing quite high, before bearing away left and entering a field. Keep along the right edge to cross a stile and continue along the left edge of

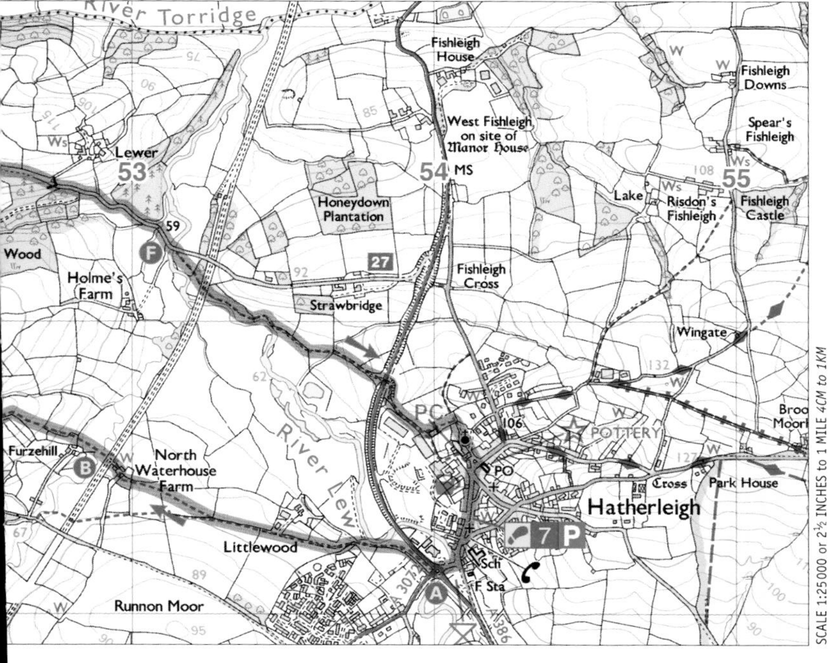

water meadows. Cross a footbridge and walk along a fenced path, crossing a stile, onto a tarmac way, which passes under the A386. Cross another stile; at the entrance to Hatherleigh Market bear left over a stile to a footpath junction.

Turn left; leave the trees and walk along the edge of a meadow, turning right to find St John the Baptist Church, most of which dates from the 14th and 15th centuries. Its shingled spire – which crashed through the roof in storms in January 1990, and has since been rebuilt – is a local landmark. Pass the church to reach the square: note the National School (1938) right and the impressive cow and sheep head sculptures, which mark the devastating foot and mouth outbreak in 2001. Turn right down Market Street, which leads into Bridge Street (passing the **Hatherleigh Tearooms**) and the car park. ●

The River Lew

Roadford Lake & Germansweek

Start	Southweek Cross, Germansweek
Distance	5¼ miles (8.3km)
Height gain	540 feet (165m)
Approximate time	2½ hours
Parking	Lay-by at Southweek Cross; follow signs for Germansweek from Roadford Lake or A3079; Germansweek is 9 miles west of Okehampton
Route terrain	Undulating woodland, farmland, tracks, lakeside path
Dog friendly	To be kept on leads through farmland and lakeside path
Ordnance Survey maps	Landranger 190 (Bude & Clovelly), Explorer 112 (Launceston & Holsworthy)

GPS waypoints

- Start: SX 436 929
- A: SX 438 941
- B: SX 440 943
- C: SX 446 941
- D: SX 449 938
- E: SX 447 926
- F: SX 437 923

At 730 acres Roadford Lake is the southwest's largest area of inland water. This walk starts on the quiet north-western shore – a Local Nature Reserve for overwintering birds – and explores its remote hinterland, including Germansweek, one of the smallest parishes in the county: much of it disappeared when the Wolf Valley was flooded to create the reservoir.

(Start) Cross the bridge; immediately turn right over a ladder-stile and through a gate on a narrow woodland path, which bears left uphill to meet a fence, and passes through a small gate. Wind through woodland and past a field to cross a stile; bear diagonally right uphill, aiming for a stile at the top of the field. Follow a rough path through woodland, eventually crossing a footbridge and ascending between banks (very wet in winter). The path reaches the Church of St Germanus, much restored in the 1870s; keep ahead to the lane in Germansweek, which – due its remote location – has something of a 'forgotten' feel. References in the *Domesday Book* confirm its pastoral emphasis as far back as the 11th century: *wick* (as in Southweek and Germansweek) means 'dairy-farm'. Seccombe Farm, now overlooking the lake, has been lived in by the Seccombe family since the 13th century.

Turn right **A** to pass The Old Schoolhouse, Old Paul's Shop, the quaint village hall and a house called Poet's Tenement – signs of more active times. Pass the telephone box; take the next turning right **B** (public footpath), opposite The Old Chapel (now a home). Pass houses at Bidlake; the lane reduces to a track between high banks and drops steeply to cross a small ford (footbridge). Pass a footpath junction and cross a ford (the River Wolf) on a

Roadford Lake, with Bodmin Moor beyond

double-railed footbridge to reach a crossroads of paths C. Keep straight ahead on a narrow path that climbs steeply through dense woodland, parts overgrown underfoot in summer. At the top cross a stile into a huge field. The footpath arrow points half right, but the right of way runs half left to reach a gate (footpath post) onto a lane.

Turn left D; 200 yds later turn right on a rough hedged track. Where that bends sharp left towards Redstone Farm keep ahead through a metal gate (blue arrow). Follow the right edge of the field, soon passing through a gate in a fence (if this area is blocked bear left through a gate, then right along the fence, soon bearing right along the top edge of the field). Look ahead for views of the reservoir dam and beyond to Bodmin Moor, and left towards Dartmoor. Pass through a gate at the end of the field; descend gently in the same direction and through another (the field boundaries on the OS map do not tie up with those on the ground through this section). Follow the right edge of the next huge marshy field, with a line of oaks right. Pass through a gate at the end; bear slightly left across the next (as signed), aiming for a bridlepath post on a hedgebank corner which comes into view.

At the bridlepath fork turn right E; follow the hedgebank to the field end, bearing left through a gate. Turn right along a wire fence, with rough ground (West Moor) beyond; where the fence shoots off right at 90 degrees keep straight across the field, aiming for a hedgebank corner (blue arrow). Keep the hedgebank left (boggy and uneven in winter) to meet a track; follow it gently downhill through gates (often open) – with good views of the lake and bridge ahead –to meet the road F.

For your car turn right; but better to cross over through a bridlegate on a rough track, heading towards the lake. Where the track leads into a field pass through a gate to its right down a hedged track, wet underfoot at times. A gate leads to a T-junction; turn right. This level grassy path, with glimpses of

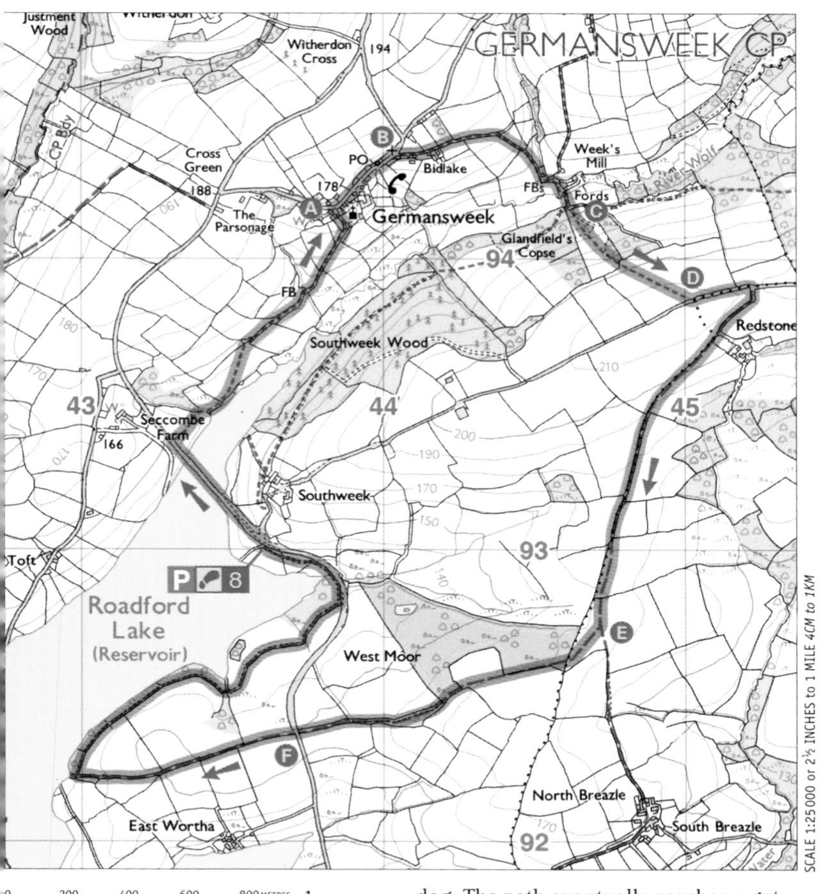

0 200 400 600 800 METRES 1 KILOMETRES
0 200 400 600 YARDS ½ MILES

the lake through trees, eventually passes through a gate into an area of culm grassland, a haven for butterflies and wildflowers, and a globally rare wildlife habitat. Research has shown that – quite apart from its appeal for birdwatchers – Roadford has a healthy population of hazel dormice, present before the valley was flooded in 1989. At the time of writing plans were afoot to graze Highland cattle here, so take care if you have a dog. The path eventually reaches a gate at the end of the parking area. For refreshments go to the **Lakeside Café** (Pay and Display) near the dam at the south end of the lake. ●

Village hall and war memorial, Germansweek

Braunton Marsh & Burrows

Start	Velator Quay, Braunton
Distance	6¼ miles (10km)
Height gain	Negligible
Approximate time	2½ hours
Parking	Free parking at Velator Quay; Velator/Braunton Burrows signed off A361 on the Barnstaple side of Braunton
Route terrain	Level coastal path, field tracks, country lanes; note no shade on route
Dog friendly	Non-dog friendly stiles on Coast Path along River Caen
Ordnance Survey maps	Landranger 180 (Barnstaple & Ilfracombe), Explorer 139 (Bideford, Ilfracombe & Barnstaple)

GPS waypoints

- Start: SS 484 354
- A SS 480 344
- B SS 469 330
- C SS 464 326
- D SS 464 355
- E SS 474 357
- F SS 476 355
- G SS 484 359

This lengthy yet level walk explores the heart of the North Devon Biosphere Reserve, designated in 2002 on account of the area's rare plants and continuous human use from ancient times. The Coast Path follows the River Caen to meet the Taw; the return passes Braunton Burrows, one of Europe's most important dune systems, and traverses Braunton's medieval Great Field.

Velator Quay – today the haunt of pleasure craft – dates from 1853, when deepening of the River Caen enabled ships of up to 130 tons to access it. It was a thriving port, and an important lime-burning centre, until the arrival of the railway in 1874.

Embankments constructed in the 19th century to protect Braunton Marshes from the influx of tidal waters today provide pleasant walking routes; pick up the Coast Path from the southern end of the parking area (by the information board) and follow it along the embankment above the River Caen, soon crossing a stone stile. Cross another by the tollhouse (the road to Broad Sands below right is private), and keep ahead, with tidal mudflats left and views over the marshes to the right – grazing cattle, yellow flags, small stone linhays (shelters for livestock) – and glimpses of the dunes of Braunton Burrows, in places rising to almost 100ft high, beyond.

Reach a footpath junction A at the north end of Horsey Island (an area of reclaimed marshland); follow the Coast Path (left fork), soon crossing a stile, and later a stone one as the River Caen meets the River Taw. The Coast Path bears right, with increasingly good views across the Taw/Torridge confluence to Appledore.

A long straight stretch, with views to the beach at Broad Sands ahead, leads to the White House (landing place for the old Appledore ferry); turn right on the Coast Path to meet a lane B. *It is possible at low tide to walk along the beach, eventually turning right through the parking area to rejoin the recommended route at the entrance to Braunton Burrows. For a shorter walk altogether turn right at* Ⓑ *and follow the lane back to* Ⓐ. Turn left and walk through a broad parking area, passing an information board at the end to enter Braunton Burrows, internationally renowned on account of its rare and diverse flora and fauna: Braunton parish boasts more species of flowering plant than any other in England. Follow the track ahead through low-growing vegetation to meet a Coast Path post.

Turn right Ⓒ and follow the track for

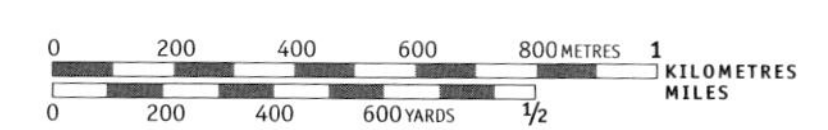

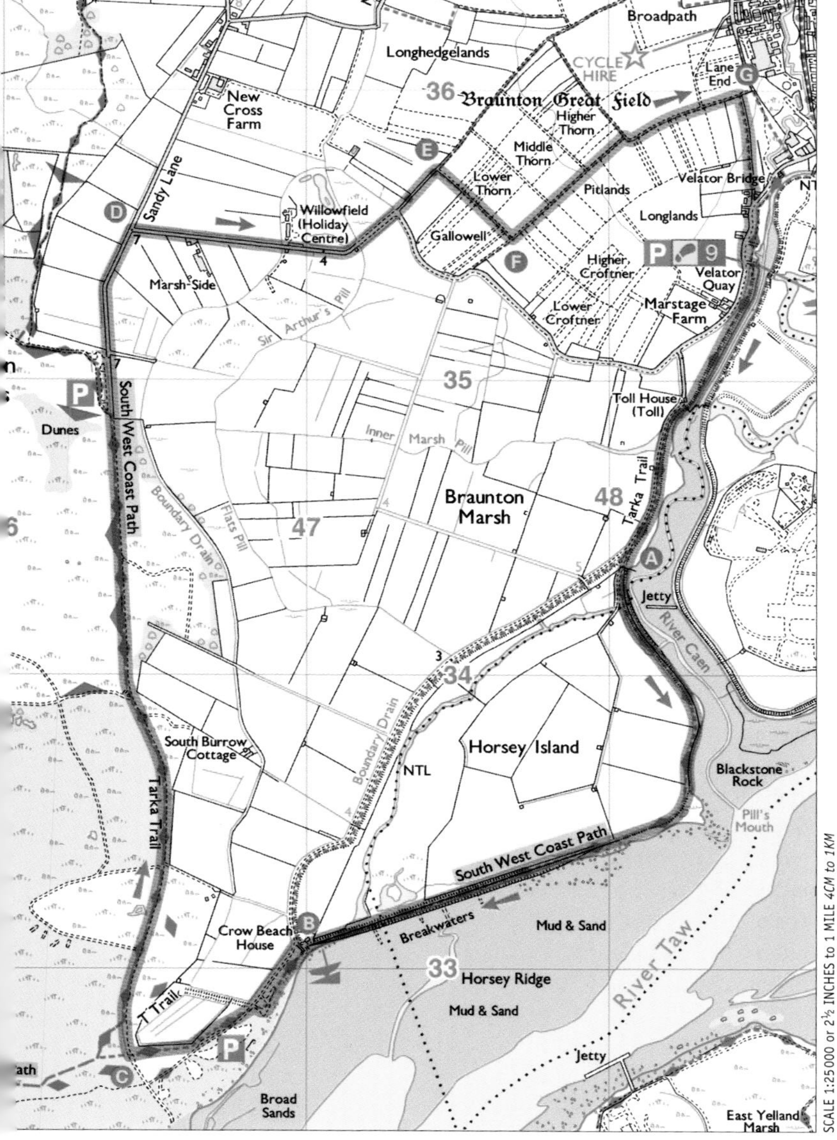

about 1¼ miles between the dunes and marshes. Originally the old way to the ferry, this track – known as 'the American Road' – was widened and straightened in the Second World War when the area was used for military amphibious training exercises in preparation for D-Day. Today it is the least interesting part of this walk; look out for cyclists (this section is both Coast Path and Tarka Trail). Pass an area of open water (left), beyond which the Coast Path is signed left; keep straight ahead to pass a parking area, and onto Sandy Lane.

Take the first lane right Ⓓ. You find yourself in a very un-Devon landscape: a lane running straight ahead across Braunton Marsh, more reminiscent of the Somerset Levels! Pass Willowfield Lake Cottages, soon after bearing left on the lane to cross Sir Arthur's Pill (drainage channel). At the next right bend keep ahead up a hedged track; 200 yds later turn right Ⓔ on a public footpath and walk along the right edge of a field. At the next footpath junction turn left Ⓕ and follow a track through the middle of Braunton Great Field – a remnant of the medieval open strip field system, with many field names dating from that time – to reach a T-junction of tracks. Turn right, immediately bearing left on the track as it heads across the field towards houses on the edge of Braunton.

About 50 yds before the end of the field turn right Ⓖ through a small gate (dogs on leads) and keep along the left edge of two fields. Keep ahead to the lane; turn right for the short walk to Velator Quay. ●

High water at Velator Quay

Molland church & Common

Start	Molland
Distance	5 miles (8km)
Height gain	1,100 feet (335m)
Approximate time	3 hours
Parking	Free parking at Molland church; Molland is 7½ miles east of South Molton, signed off B3227
Route terrain	Hilly fields and tracks, open common, quiet lanes; some muddy sections
Dog friendly	To be kept on leads through fields and on common; a few non-dog friendly stiles
Ordnance Survey maps	Landranger 181 (Minehead & Brendon Hills), Explorer 114 (Exeter & the Exe Valley)

GPS waypoints

Start	SS 807 283
A	SS 817 283
B	SS 819 282
C	SS 826 280
D	SS 830 293
E	SS 834 298
F	SS 827 299
G	SS 824 293
H	SS 815 291

A labyrinth of lanes leads to the remote hamlet of Molland, nestled in rolling countryside beneath Molland Common, one of the least-visited parts of southern Exmoor. This switchback walk makes good use of Exmoor's extensive bridleway network through quiet wooded valleys before climbing to Anstey Gate and taking rough paths across the common, haunt of red deer and Exmoor ponies.

St Mary's is the best-preserved Georgian church in Devon, with high box pews and three-decker pulpit, as well as a 15th-century nave and tower, unusual screen and set of stocks – and a tranquil atmosphere in keeping with its location.

From the parking area (**London Inn** and **Molland Tea Rooms** [seasonal] right) turn left along the lane and walk away from the hamlet. At Moor Lane South keep straight on, soon dropping steeply into and out of a combe. The lane bears right at Latchgate Cross: keep ahead to bear right through a gate, then turn left along the top edge of three fields. At the end of the third cross a stile into another; the right of way (ROW) leads straight ahead into a small gulley, so pick your way downhill through that, then bear left then right downhill to cross a stile onto a lane A *(the ROW varies from that marked on the OS map at this point).*

Turn left; climb steeply to a junction of lanes and tracks at Bremley Cross. Keep ahead on a tarmac way to a bridlepath junction B. Turn right to Whitley Farm, immediately passing through a gate. The switchback track eventually bears right through a gate to pass the farmhouse (left). Pass through another gate to meet a track.

Turn left C; follow the broad track (muddy in places) through grasses and bracken up the wooded Combe Valley, with the swell of Molland Common ahead. At the next bridlepath junction keep ahead over a stream on a footbridge and through a gate into woodland. At the next junction, keep ahead with fields right, towards Brimblecombe (narrow and muddy after wet weather). On reaching the house bear left then right on a rough track, which ascends steeply. The track climbs through two fields to meet a path junction via a gate/cattle-grid on the common's lower edge.

To shorten the walk turn left, and rejoin the route at Ⓖ – but to enjoy the openness of and views from Molland Common turn right Ⓓ on a track. After 200 yds where the track splits bear left uphill, and climb steadily (note a memorial stone to a hunting couple in the hedgebank right) to an embanked parking area at Anstey Gate; cross it diagonally to meet the lane in the top left corner.

Do not take the rough path that parallels the lane but turn left Ⓔ (note the bridlepath sign by the cattle-grid behind: Molland is directed sharp left) along the car park bank. Just before the bottom corner bear right (look for an arrow made of stones on the ground) on a rough grassy path that descends gently across the common, soon narrowing and becoming more distinct through an area of heather and bracken. At a vague fork keep straight ahead, descending gradually towards the head of Anstey's Combe, which runs away steeply left. At the top of the combe (gully) a rough path crosses our route.

Keep straight on for a few steps. The bridlepath continues ahead to cross boggy Gourt Mires, but to avoid that bear left Ⓕ on a rough path running south along the right edge of the combe to meet the bottom edge of the common opposite a gate.

Turn right Ⓖ, immediately dropping

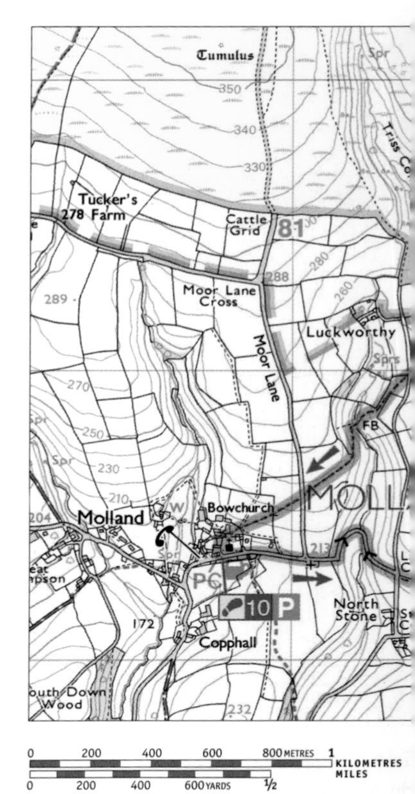

steeply to cross a stream. Follow the bottom edge of the common, eventually descending steeply on a rough track that bears right and left to cross a stream on a bridge and pass through a gate at Smallacombe Ⓗ. The track ascends to a T-junction. Keep straight ahead through a gate; bear diagonally left across the field, aiming for a fence corner. Continue in the same direction through a gate in the field corner. Cross the next field, dropping steeply across a disused leat, to cross a footbridge/stile/footbridge under trees. Ascend big steps onto a grassy track; turn left, soon bearing right uphill, with beech trees above right. Keep ahead across the field, aiming for the far left corner, and through a gate onto Moor Lane.

Cross over, ascend steps and go through a gate. Head across the next

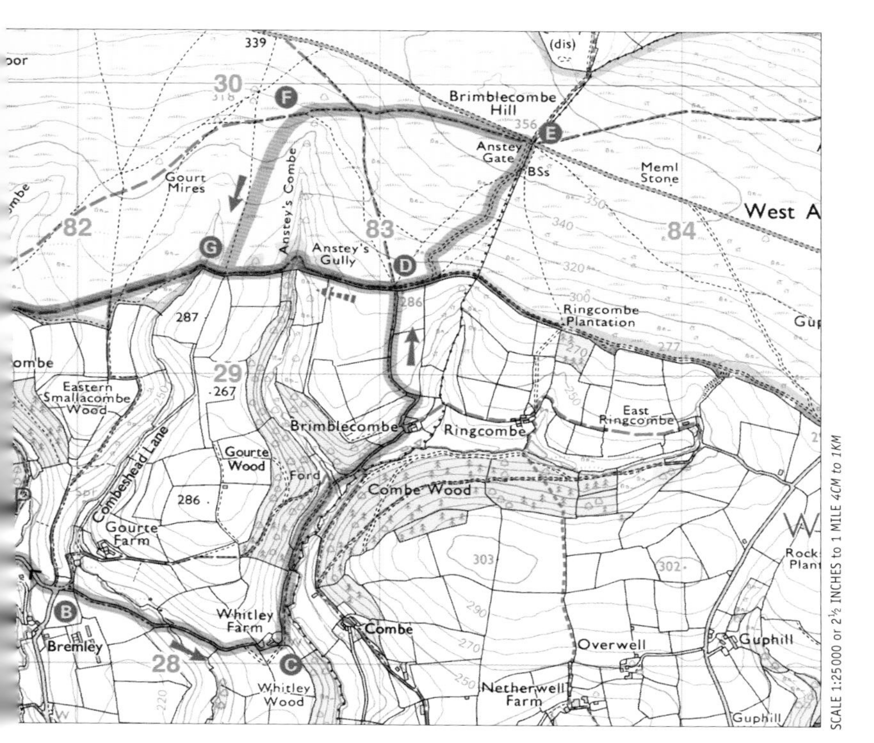

field, aiming slightly to the right of the church tower. Pass through a gate; head across the next field to pass through an open gateway with farm buildings right. Keep ahead, downhill. Just before meeting the farmhouse (right) turn left through a small gate into the churchyard. Keep ahead, turning right through the gate, then left and left again for your car. ●

Molland Common

Bampton & Morebath

Start	St Michael's Church, Bampton
Distance	5½ miles (8.8km)
Height gain	985 feet (300m)
Approximate time	3 hours
Parking	Free on-street parking, or Pay and Display car park in Bampton, 7½ miles north of Tiverton off A396
Route terrain	Undulating field paths and tracks, plus road section
Dog friendly	Dogs to be kept on leads throughout; some non-dog friendly stiles
Ordnance Survey maps	Landranger 181 (Minehead & Brendon Hills), Explorer 114 (Exeter & the Exe Valley)

GPS waypoints

- SS 956 222
- Ⓐ SS 940 238
- Ⓑ SS 944 238
- Ⓒ SS 951 249
- Ⓓ SS 955 249
- Ⓔ SS 959 236
- Ⓕ SS 962 235
- Ⓖ SS 957 225

Once an important wool and market town, Bampton's Saxon origins are evident in its street layout and almost circular churchyard, from where this pleasant excursion via fields and green lanes leads to the little hamlet of Morebath, with its unusual church tower. The return includes an unavoidable stretch along the B3190 before footpaths lead past the remnants of Bampton's motte-and-bailey castle.

From the gates at the tower (west) end of the Church of St Michael & All Angels join Station Road opposite the car park. Turn right; on meeting Luke Street cross over and turn left. Almost immediately bear right uphill on a narrower lane (High Street – the old road to Dulverton). About 100 yds after houses turn right on a drive; where it bears left keep ahead on the Exe Valley Way (EVW) through a gate into a field. Walk up the right edge, eventually dropping over a stile. Bear left on a track, downhill; where that bears right across the field continue up the left edge, aiming for a footpath post in the corner.

Cross two stiles; immediately turn right to cross another. Bear left through a tree-covered bank, then bear right uphill, keeping the bank right. Continue along the right field edge to cross a stile at the top. Walk diagonally across the next, aiming for the top left corner. Pass through a kissing-gate; keep straight across the next field, levelling off. Pass through an open gateway in the corner; bear left, and on meeting the hedgebank turn right, with hedge left. At the end of that field pass through a gate, with views towards Dulverton below Exmoor's southern slopes: the Saxon interpretation of 'settlement by the ford over the bend' seems appropriate. Descend along the right edge of the next field. Pass through a hedgebank; continue downhill towards Coldharbour Farm.

Go through a gate past stables and

through another gate. Bear left past the farmhouse and cross the drive; keep ahead on a hedged grassy track and through a gate. Descend along the left field edge, and through a gate to a lane (EVW goes left to cross the river at Exebridge, then follows the River Barle to Dulverton).

Turn right Ⓐ along the lane – an ancient trackway from Wellington to Dulverton – to reach Blight's Farm (right). Turn left Ⓑ (unsigned) on the drive to Surridge Farm. Continue uphill eventually to pass a bungalow (left); immediately turn left through a gate and cross the field diagonally, aiming to the left of buildings. Pass through a gate; head downhill along the right edge of the field, with views to Morebath, once known for its warm health-giving chalybeate springs. Pass through a gate under a huge oak tree and follow a green lane (wet in winter,

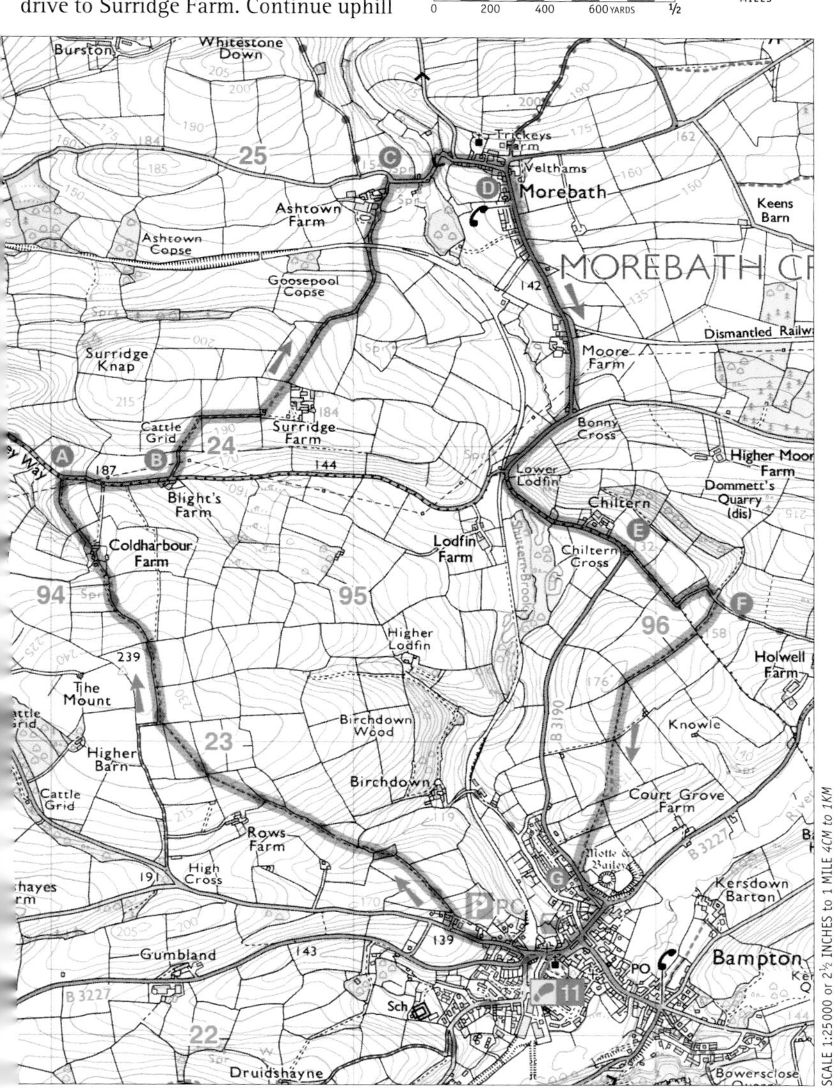

Old barns near Bampton

decked with wildflowers in summer) to meet a farm track that continues downhill across the dismantled Devon & Somerset Railway line (the Taunton–Barnstaple and Exe Valley lines met at Morebath Junction, just south of Morebath). Reach a T-junction of tracks at Ashtown Farm (of Saxon origin); bear right to a lane.

Turn right **C**; the lane drops then climbs steeply into Morebath; St George's Church sits above the lane left. The saddleback roof (the tower is 11th century) was part of 19th-century restoration, and unique in Devon. Follow the lane on to the B3190.

Turn right **D** along the road for just under 1 mile, using verges where possible. Pass Lodfin Cross, where the old railway line is visible (right). About 400 yds later the road bears sharp right; keep ahead **E** up an unsigned rising hedged track, which bears sharp left. At the crest turn right through a kissing-gate **F**. Keep along the right edge of the field. Pass through a gate and cross a stile; keep up the left edge of the next field. Go through a gate/stile combination and follow the left edge of the next. Pass through another gate; immediately turn left through another into a sloping field. Head diagonally, aiming for a gate about 20 yds left of the far right corner (old barns below left). Continue in the same direction across the next field, aiming for a gate towards the right end of the far hedge.

Cross the stile; follow a fenced path downhill. Below left are playing fields, and beyond that the wooded motte. The original castle was built in Saxon times on this vantage point – Bampton is situated at a natural crossing of the River Batherm – and fortified in the mid 11th century. Cross a stile and the next meadow; a gate leads to the road **G**.

Cross over and turn left; 75 yds later bear right down a lane. On meeting Castle Street turn right; where that bears left keep ahead along Back Street. Cross Luke Street to pass the telephone box and into the churchyard. ●

Tetcott

Start	Lana
Distance	5½ miles (8.9km)
Height gain	475 feet (145m)
Approximate time	3 hours
Parking	Laneside parking near the telephone box in Lana; Tetcott is 5 miles south of Holsworthy, signed off A388
Route terrain	Hilly fields and tracks, quiet lanes, parkland; some wet and muddy sections all year round
Dog friendly	To be kept on leads through fields and estate lands; horses in fields at Yeo Farm
Ordnance Survey maps	Landranger 190 (Bude & Clovelly), Explorer 112 (Launceston & Holsworthy)

GPS waypoints

- SX 339 963 (start)
- Ⓐ SX 344 963
- Ⓑ SX 360 951
- Ⓒ SX 334 946
- Ⓓ SX 328 958
- Ⓔ SX 330 966

An unexpected find in Devon's western Heartland: the historic Tetcott estate, acquired in the mid-1500s by John Arscott, now in the hands of the Molesworth-St Aubyns. The manor house dates from that time, and the church from the 13th century. This tranquil walk explores some of the old estate and the remote valley of the Tamar Valley, bordering Cornwall.

Pass the village shop (open some mornings) and walk towards the crossroads at Tetcott Village Cross. Follow the narrow lane ahead gently downhill to reach Lana Bridge.

Cross the bridge; turn right Ⓐ through a metal gate onto a hedged track. At the bottom (muddy) cross a small ford; pass through a gate. Bear diagonally left uphill, aiming for the top left corner of the field. Pass through the left of two gates; keep straight across the next field, aiming for the far right corner on the edge of woodland. Pass through a gate and cross a small stream (boggy); walk along the right edge of the next field, climbing gently. At the end bear right through a hedge gap, then bear left along the left edge of the next field. Pass through a gate at the end (muddy); continue along the left edge. Pass through a gate at Yendon Farm (formerly Hendon, 'high hill'); after 20 yds at a footpath post bear slightly left to pass through a gate with a dilapidated corrugated iron building right. Keep straight ahead (farmhouse right) along the drive to pass through a gate and by more buildings. At a T-junction bear right through another gate onto an open stretch with views towards Bodmin Moor (part of the same granite sheet that forms Dartmoor and the Isles of Scilly).

The track meets the A388; turn immediately right Ⓑ through the gate to Yeo Farm. Pass the house and continue through a gate onto a track, with fields right. Pass through two gates and along the right edge of the next field. At the end cross a stream and go through a gate (wet underfoot), then mount a bank on rough steps. Follow the right edge of the next field (uneven); pass through a hedgebank and keep along the right edge of the next, descending gently. A gate leads to a track on a bend; keep ahead to the lane at Luffincott Shop (the house opposite was the old smithy).

Cross over and follow the quiet lane to reach Luffincott Barton, an estate farm dating from the mid-1800s: keep ahead. As the farmhouse comes into view turn right C through an open gateway, to pass an open-fronted barn. Luffincott church (medieval in origin but rebuilt in the 1700s and no longer used: a rare example of a Georgian church) comes into view across a meadow left. Follow the grassy track downhill through a gate into a field that drops away steeply right. Keep along the top edge with the hedge left; continue ahead downhill where that bears away left (boggy underfoot) to pass a strip of trees and through a gate into woodland.

Follow the path as it bears right across a very wet section on timber cross-sections, ending at a footbridge and gate. Follow the wire fence ahead to meet a track; turn left, soon bearing right towards Mill Wood. Bear right off the track through a gate; immediately bear left on a narrow path (wet in places) along the lower edge of the wood, with glimpses of the River Tamar through the trees left. The path passes a derelict building (formerly the site of the estate's corn mill) and rises to join the mill's access track; continue along it (note the old mill leat below right). Eventually the track meets a T-junction at the end of the wood.

View across the fields to Tetcott Manor and Holy Cross Church

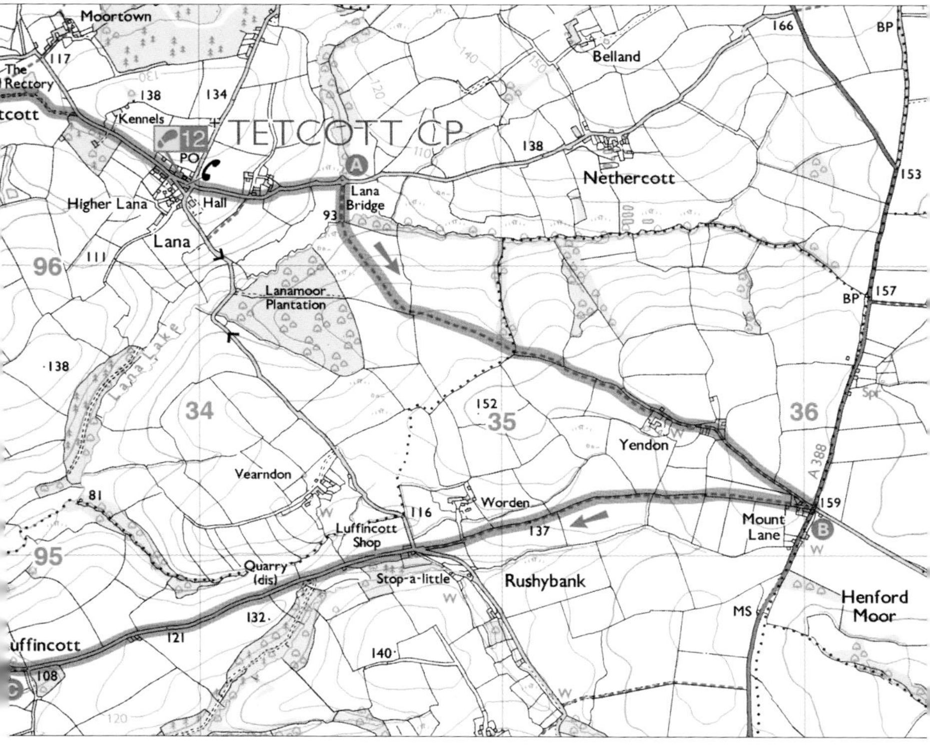

0 200 400 600 800 METRES 1 KILOMETRES
0 200 400 600 YARDS ½ MILES

SCALE 1:25000 or 2½ INCHES to 1 MILE 4CM to 1KM

Turn left D on a broad track that descends gently, then bears right to meet another; climb steadily towards Tetcott, bearing sharp left as the church comes into view to pass farm buildings. Head for two fine 18th-century gateposts; just before reaching them turn sharp right E past a stilted 18th-century brick granary. Follow the track towards Holy Cross Church, passing through a gate and bearing sharp left between buildings to find Tetcott Manor left. The last of the Arscotts to live here – John (1718–88) – was something of a character and kept a dwarf jester, Black John, said to haunt the manor to this day! Turn right for Holy Cross Church; continue past the church through a lychgate to reach the manor drive. Turn right through a gate by a cattle-grid and follow the drive across beautiful parkland ('The Wilderness'), to meet the lane by another fine set of gateposts dating from the early 1700s.

Turn right to return to Lana.

Codden Hill

Start	Village hall, Landkey
Distance	5¾ miles (9km)
Height gain	820 feet (250m)
Approximate time	3 hours
Parking	Free parking behind The Castle pub (opposite village hall); Landkey is signed off A361 1 mile southeast of Barnstaple
Route terrain	Undulating lanes, open fields, hedged tracks; steady climb to Codden Hill
Dog friendly	To be kept on leads in farmland
Ordnance Survey maps	Landranger 180 (Barnstaple & Ilfracombe), Explorer 139 (Bideford, Ilfracombe & Barnstaple)

GPS waypoints

- Start: SS 597 310
- A: SS 595 305
- B: SS 591 298
- C: SS 588 294
- D: SS 572 296
- E: SS 571 301
- F: SS 584 307
- G: SS 589 311

Codden Hill stands 620ft above the Taw Valley, and affords magnificent 360-degree views over the Taw–Torridge Estuary and surrounding countryside. A long steady climb to the Monument is followed by a more gradual descent and pleasant return through fields and woods. There is one short but very steep, scrambly downhill section of path to the lane at the bottom of Codden Hill.

Facing **The Castle**, turn right along Blake's Hill Road. Take the first lane right (Mill Road), signed Tarka Trail, soon crossing Mill Bridge; immediately turn right up a narrow lane and climb steadily past buildings at Newland Park. At the T-junction take the right fork; cross the lane (A) and pass through a metal gate on a public footpath. The path bears right and climbs steadily uphill. At the top of the field go through another gate; continue half right uphill to cross a stile in a wire fence. Bear diagonally left uphill, aiming for a stile in the hedge: Codden Hill appears ahead right. Keep straight across the next field, and in the top right corner cross a stile onto a lane.

Turn left downhill to reach a junction at Bableigh Cross (B): keep ahead downhill (dead end). Pass the entrance to Pitt Farm; bear slightly left on a

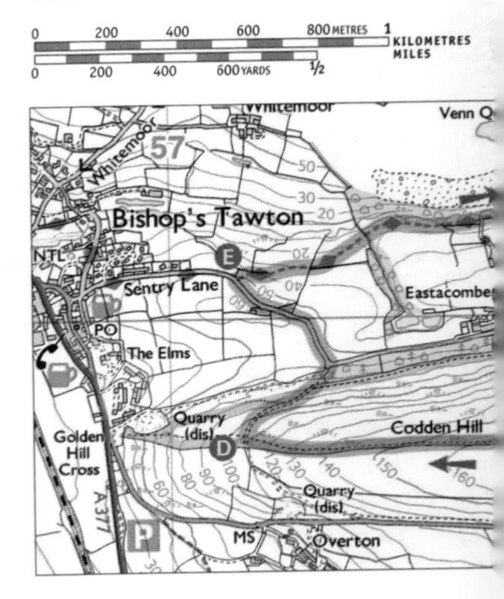

hedged track. Curve sharp right and climb steeply uphill. At the top bear left to a parking area (right) **C**; bear right through it to pass through a gate on a public footpath. Follow a broad track gently uphill, with views to Landkey right. Where the track forks keep ahead, with a hedge left; on meeting a gate on the left keep ahead, now in open grassland, with a fence left. Pass through a gate to reach the monument on the hilltop, dedicated to Caroline, wife of Jeremy Thorpe MP, who lived at Cobbaton. Engraved around the perimeter are the points of the compass and an indication of what you might see from this excellent viewpoint: Lundy, Exmoor, Dartmoor, Bodmin Moor and Hartland Point.

Pass to the right of the monument and through a small gate; keep ahead, gently downhill, along a fence. Drop to meet a crossroads of tracks and turn right **D**. The track runs along the side of the hill, eventually dropping more steeply and bearing right. Where another track comes in from the left – and our track runs straight ahead – look for a narrower track that descends very steeply, with a wire fence right, and turn left *(take care: firmer ground can be found towards the left)*. Meet another track; turn right through a gate to meet a lane on a corner.

Turn left along the lane. After about 400 yds, where it bears left, turn right **E** over a stile. Meet a hedge corner, then keep straight across the field, aiming for a hedge gap. In the next field bear diagonally left downhill, aiming for a stile (and stream) just past a telegraph pole. In the next field bear left across the corner then keep along the left edge, with the river left. Towards the end of the field the path enters woodland, soon passing through a kissing-gate and along a boardwalk (look out for herons). Reach a kissing-gate at a footpath junction; keep ahead through another. The track reduces to a

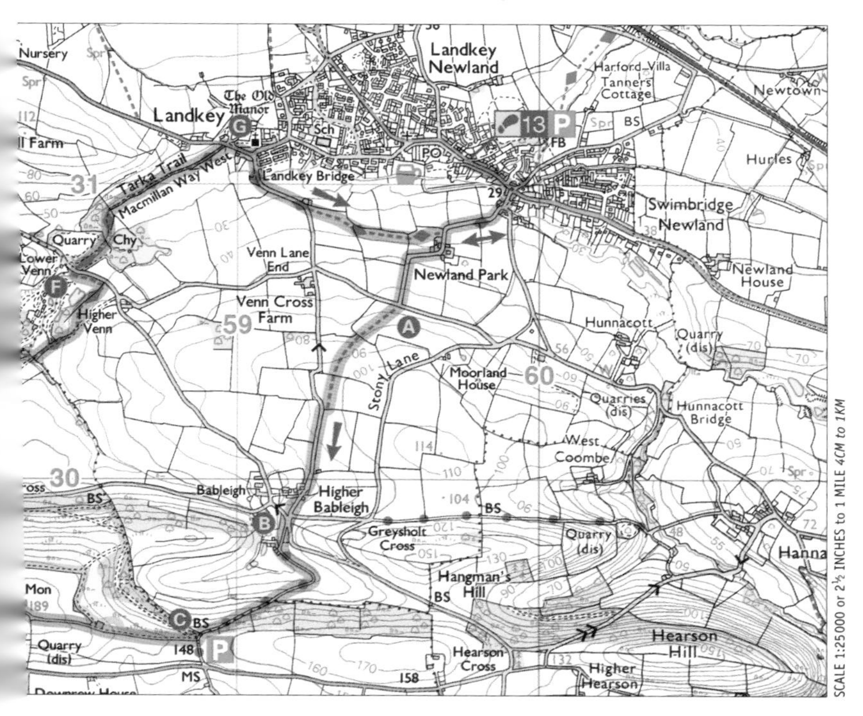

path and ascends along the top edge of woodland.

Emerge into a field via a kissing-gate; keep ahead, soon turning left along a track. Cross a bridge over Venn Quarry (in the 18th century the area's most important source of lime, used in mortar, in limewash and as fertiliser). Rare mazzard trees (related to the cherry and unique to North Devon) have been planted around the quarry. The path eventually bears left to cross a stile, then drops steeply to a lane. Turn left over the river.

Just over the bridge turn right F through a kissing-gate. Walk through woodland, eventually passing through a gate, and follow a fenced path towards Landkey, reaching a lane via a gate. Turn right G to pass late 15th-century St Paul's Church (the **Ring o' Bells** pub is just past the church). The church contains memorials to the Acland family, one of Devon's greatest, who originated at Acland Barton to the north of the village.

Take the first lane right signed to the Tarka Trail (Bableigh Road). Cross the river again; where the lane bears right bear left by a cottage over a stile by a gate. Keep along the left edge of three fields to cross a stile onto a lane, rejoining the outward route. Turn left; at the junction turn left over Mill Bridge to reach the road through Landkey. Turn left for the village hall. ●

On the summit of Codden Hill

Sheepwash & Buckland Filleigh

Start	Sheepwash
Distance	6¼ miles (10.1km)
Height gain	525 feet (160m)
Approximate time	3 hours
Parking	The Square, Sheepwash (free): Sheepwash is 5 miles from Hatherleigh, signed off A3072 at Highampton
Route terrain	Fields, green lanes, woodland tracks, quiet lanes
Dog friendly	To be kept on leads through farmland; non-dog friendly stiles
Ordnance Survey maps	Landrangers 191 (Okehampton & North Dartmoor) and 190 (Bude & Clovelly), Explorers 112 (Launceston & Holsworthy) and 126 (Clovelly & Hartland)

GPS waypoints

- SS 486 063
- Ⓐ SS 486 067
- Ⓑ SS 472 093
- Ⓒ SS 465 093
- Ⓓ SS 461 088
- Ⓔ SS 467 071
- Ⓕ SS 476 075

The delightful village of Sheepwash, on a hill above the River Torridge, is a long way from anywhere – 10 miles from Holsworthy, 12 from Torrington – and has a distinctly agricultural feel. This is a good introduction to aspects of much of Devon's unspoilt Heartland: stock in fields, crops planted over footpaths, muddy and rough sections ... and you won't see a soul!

From Sheepwash Cross walk along the lane signed Petrockstowe, to pass the PO/Community Stores and enter a truly rural area of rolling fields, pockets of woodland and scattered working farms. Just past the entrance to North Road Farm turn left over a stile into a field Ⓐ. Bear right up the right edge of three fields (wet gateways) to cross a stile. The ROW heads straight across the next field, about 50 yds from the right hedge, dropping to cross a stream via a stile/footbridge/stile. Walk up the left edge of the next field; on reaching a metal gate left, and barns, turn left through a small gate, then right up a concrete track past farm buildings (Swardicott Farm) to the lane. *For a really short walk turn left along the lane to Upcott Barton* Ⓕ.

Cross the lane to pass through a small gate and follow a rough green lane that climbs gently, eventually bearing right through a gate before dropping past Lake Farm. When level with the farmhouse follow the track left; at the next junction keep straight on, dropping gently. Pass remote cottages, then Buckland Mill. Follow the track over Mussel Brook into woodland. The track bears right (private track to Modbury left), soon passes a derelict building (left) and eventually meets a lane by a huge oak tree.

Sheepwash village seen across the fields

Turn left B; walk steadily uphill. The lane levels off and enters open country; at the entrance to Buckland House turn left on the drive C. The estate came to the Filleighs (hence Buckland Filleigh) in 1454 and was held by them until the 1840s. The present house – a rather austere early Georgian mansion – was much altered in 1810 after a fire. Where the drive bears right to the house turn left; on meeting a fence corner turn right, and enter the churchyard of St Mary and Holy Trinity via the lychgate. Parts date from the 13th century or earlier, but extensive restoration took place in Victorian times. At the south door turn left; leave the churchyard over a stile into parkland. Follow a mown path downhill to cross a footbridge at the right end of the lake. Turn right on another mown path through wildflower meadows and climb gently uphill through young plantations, with views to the house right. The path crosses others, but keep straight on, eventually levelling off to meet a lane opposite Glebe Cottages.

Turn left D along the lane, which rises gently and gains wonderful views of Dartmoor's northwest corner. The lane passes a cottage at Woodhead – sadly the footpath signed left cannot be recommended – so a long walk on the lane (1½ miles) is unavoidable. Luckily it is very quiet and more like a well-surfaced footpath! Turn left at Down Cross E.

At Upcott Barton turn right F through a gateway on a concrete drive, passing between buildings. At the end of the drive turn right as signed through a gate into a field; bear slightly left to pass a footpath post, and keep ahead to meet the hedge. Turn left along it, downhill, with views across fields to Sheepwash. At the bottom of the field cross a stile into damp rough grassland; push straight ahead towards a line of big oak trees to find a stepped footbridge over a stream. Keep ahead through a strip of woodland to emerge over a stile into a field. Bear left along the left edge, bearing right uphill on meeting a line of oaks on a bank, soon passing a footpath post. Keep in the same direction past clumps of oak. Just after a gap in the bank bear slightly left past a footpath post onto a rough downhill track, with bank and trees right. Pass through a gate and cross a

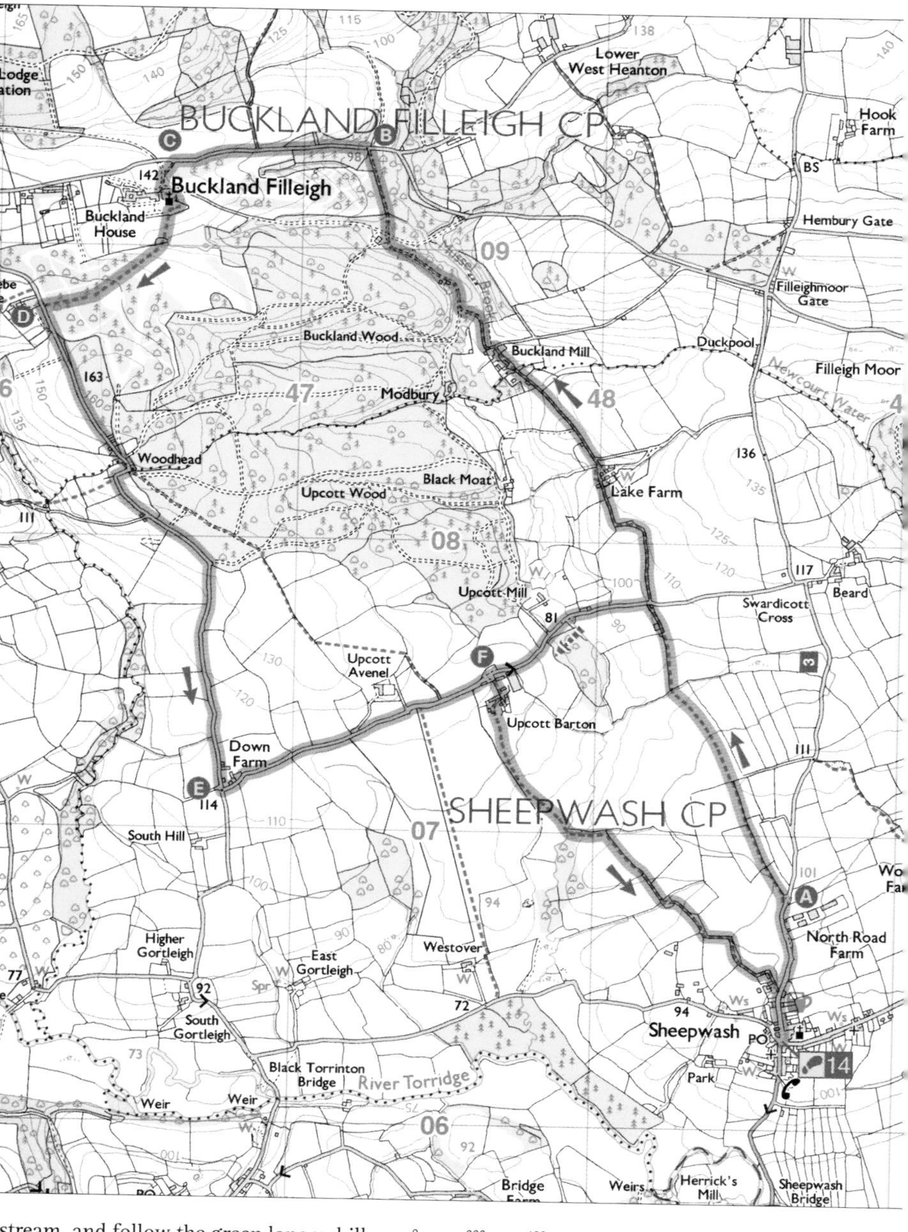

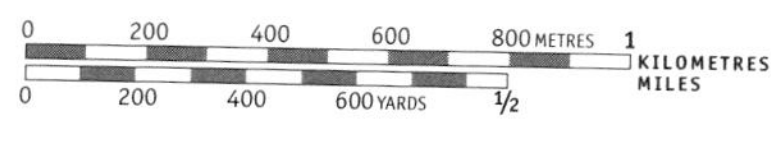

stream, and follow the green lane uphill, eventually bearing right through a gate, then another onto the drive to Old Court; pass through a gate onto the lane.

Turn right for The Square and refreshment at **The Half Moon Inn**. Sheepwash is bordered by several watercourses, and it is thought that the name derives from the practice of washing sheep before shearing. The Church of St Lawrence, which overlooks The Square, was rebuilt in 1880 after a fire.

Woody Bay & The Beacon

Start	Woody Bay
Distance	5¾ miles (9km)
Height gain	1,410 feet (430m)
Approximate time	3½ hours
Parking	Free NT car park; follow signs for Woody Bay from A39 at Martinhoe Cross just east of Woody Bay Station, between Parracombe and Barbrook
Route terrain	Non-rocky Coast Path, long steady ascents and descents, some damp areas in coastal woodland
Ordnance Survey maps	Landranger 180 (Barnstaple & Ifracombe), Explorer OL9 Exmoor

GPS waypoints

- Start: SS 675 486
- A: SS 673 486
- B: SS 655 481
- C: SS 654 487
- D: SS 671 490

Both outward and return routes of this circular walk stick to the coast using both Coast Path and a Victorian carriage drive with magnificent views along Exmoor's cliffs and plentiful opportunities for spotting a good variety of seabirds.

From the parking area walk uphill; where the lane soon bears sharp left keep straight ahead **A** onto a broad track, a former late Victorian carriageway (see later), signed to **Hunters Inn**. The track runs along the top of West Woodybay Wood, a designated SAC (Special Area of Conservation) for its sessile (hanging) oakwoods; the National Trust is doing extensive work in the Woody Bay area to control the spread of rhododendron, which can be seen dotting the cliffs later in this walk. The drive passes through a small gate and soon enters open country, dropping into the combe of the Hollow Brook and soon returning to the cliffs. Look out for a small path rising left to the site of The Beacon, a small round fort occupied from c AD50–74 by a garrison of 80 Roman soldiers on the lookout for attack from the Silures of South Wales.

Follow the track on eventually to meet the edge of Heddon's Mouth Cleave, and turn inland, with stunning views over the steep-sided wooded valley ahead; the Coast Path to Combe Martin runs 500ft above the other side of the Cleave. The track descends gently, crossing Hill Brook, and continues to descend to meet a junction of paths **B**. *For an ice cream from the NT shop or refreshments at The Hunters Inn (see Walk 20) keep straight ahead.*

To continue turn sharp right, following the bridleway, which descends towards the Heddon River. Undulate along the right bank, keeping left at a fork along a pretty riverside path, to meet a bridge and the Coast Path **C**. Do not cross the river, but follow the track straight ahead. The track ascends slightly as the landscape starts to open up; reach a junction and bear right on the Coast Path, signed Woody Bay, on a narrow path that ascends steadily up the east side of the valley. Pass through an area of bracken and cross Hill Brook. Soon the beach at rocky Heddon's Mouth – a rare inlet on this inhospitable coast – and the restored 19th-century double limekiln, last used in 1870, comes into view below. Charcoal and gorse were burned in the lower chamber, with limestone and culm (from South Wales) layered above, to produce quicklime, used to fertilise Exmoor's acid soils. The beach was last used commercially in the Second World War for the export of timber which was used in the mines of South Wales.

Reach Highveer Point and enjoy wonderful views west along the coast towards Widmouth Head near Ilfracombe and east to The Foreland beyond Lynmouth. The Coast Path – this section remarkably even underfoot – runs east towards Little and then Great Burland Rocks, then drops past the 656ft waterfall in Hollow Brook Combe (wet underfoot) to gain spectacular views over the rocky coastal formations at Wringapeak (look for razorbills and guillemots in summer), with Woody Bay and Gothic Lee Abbey *(see Walk 5)* beyond. Woody Bay has an interesting history: Martinhoe Manor estate was bought by 'Colonel' Benjamin Greene Lake in 1885, who planned to turn it into an upmarket resort but he went bankrupt and was imprisoned for fraud, and the estate was purchased by the National Trust in 1965.

The Coast Path enters West Woodybay Wood, soon passing through a gate, and eventually meets a lane on a hairpin bend just above Martinhoe Manor (originally Wooda Bay House, built in 1859). The Coast Path bears left downhill; take the right fork D and follow the lane uphill, climbing steadily to reach a T-junction. Turn right to the parking area.

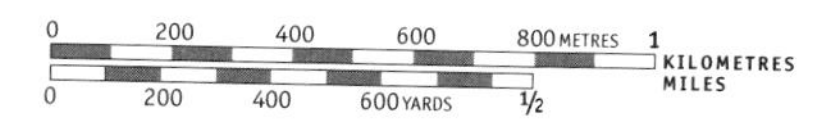

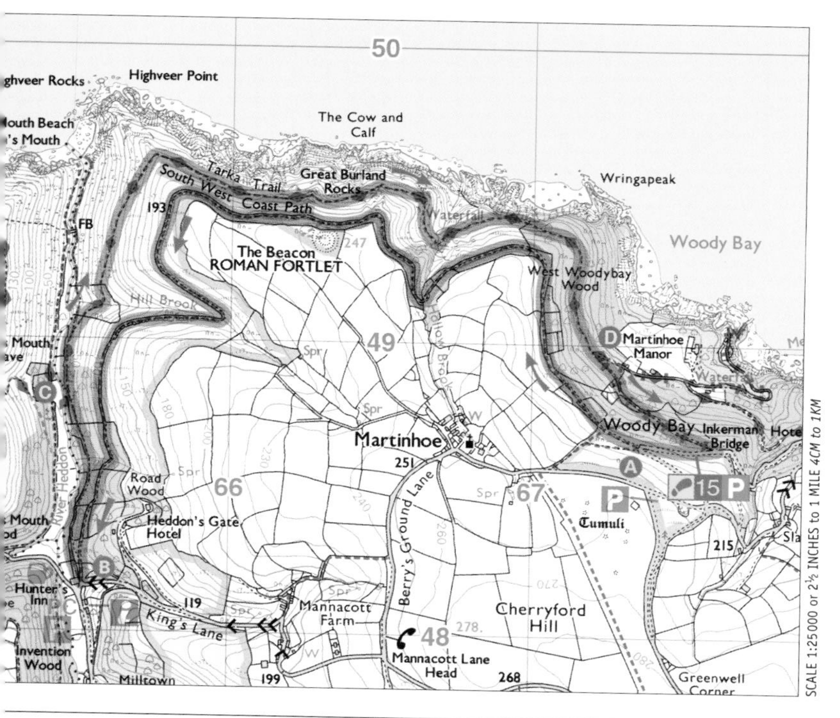

Brownsham & Clovelly

Start	Brownsham
Distance	6¾ miles (10.7km)
Height gain	1,525 feet (465m)
Approximate time	3½ hours
Parking	NT car park at Brownsham (free) 2 miles northeast of Hartland; follow signs for Hartland Point from Lighthouse Cross B3248, then for Brownsham
Route terrain	Woodland tracks, fields lanes, Coast Path; steady ascents/descents
Dog friendly	To be kept on leads through farmland and estate; pheasants and stock
Ordnance Survey maps	Landranger 190 (Bude & Clovelly), Explorer 126 (Clovelly & Hartland)

GPS waypoints

- Start SS 285 259
- A SS 297 259
- B SS 309 249
- C SS 310 244
- D SS 316 249
- E SS 315 250
- F SS 301 263
- G SS 290 264

This walk visits one of North Devon's hotspots – the cliff-side village of Clovelly – via a relatively easy route from Brownsham, best walked in May when bluebells flood the wooded Coast Path. An open section across Gallantry Bower – site of a Bronze Age barrow – affords lovely coastal views, as does a short excursion to The Lookout above Mouthmill Beach.

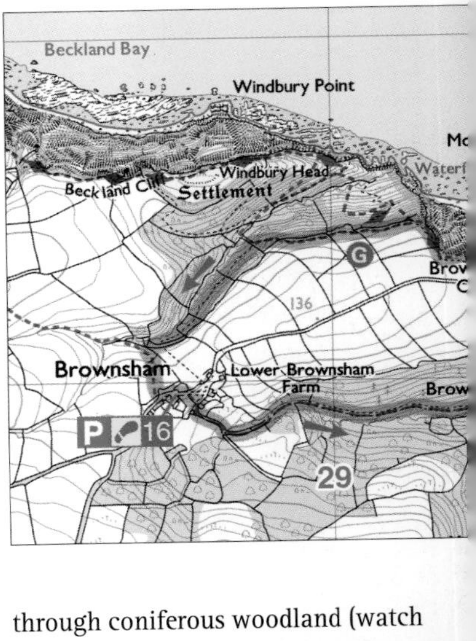

From the car park turn left along a track. At the junction with restored farm buildings opposite turn right on a track that soon curves left, passes through a gate/stile, then descends steadily through woodland to meet a fork: keep ahead (right fork) to cross a stream and reach a T-junction.

Turn left A; after 200 yds bear right on a stony track that climbs steeply through coniferous woodland (watch out for pheasants). Pass through a gate into a field; bear left along the lower edge. At the top pass through a gate into a field; bear half right uphill, passing a lone gate and continuing to pass through another onto a track at the top; bear left, soon passing through a gate. The level track eventually descends past Court Farm; note disused limekilns left. Follow the farm drive past a link to the Coast Path and continue gently uphill through fields to Clovelly Court, with restored 15th-century All Saints Church ahead. The drive bears right along a lime avenue: just round the bend take a track that soon bears left to the gates of Clovelly Court Garden (honesty box: for the church turn left through the lychgate). The original mansion at Clovelly Court – the ancestral home of the owners of Clovelly – was built in 1681; the estate was bought by the Hamlyn family in 1740, and the house remodelled first in Georgian and later Gothic style after extensive fire damage. Turn right along a path to meet the road (B3237) on a bend by a gatehouse **B**.

If you wish to shorten the walk turn left downhill for ½ mile to rejoin the route at **E**. Walk up the road with care, climbing steadily to Higher Clovelly: turn left for Wrinkleberry **C** to pass the primary school, then follow ancient Wrinkleberry Lane, which narrows, becomes cobbled and descends steeply to the top of Clovelly village, joining the Coast Path. The author Charles Kingsley lived in Clovelly while his father was rector. *Westward Ho!* published in 1855, brought Clovelly – a small herring-fishing village clinging to the steep cliffs – to the world's attention. Today it is worth a visit, but best in the quiet of early morning or evening.

Turn left **D** (Coast Path) to pass Mount Pleasant, with benches and

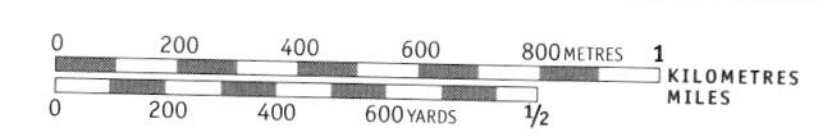

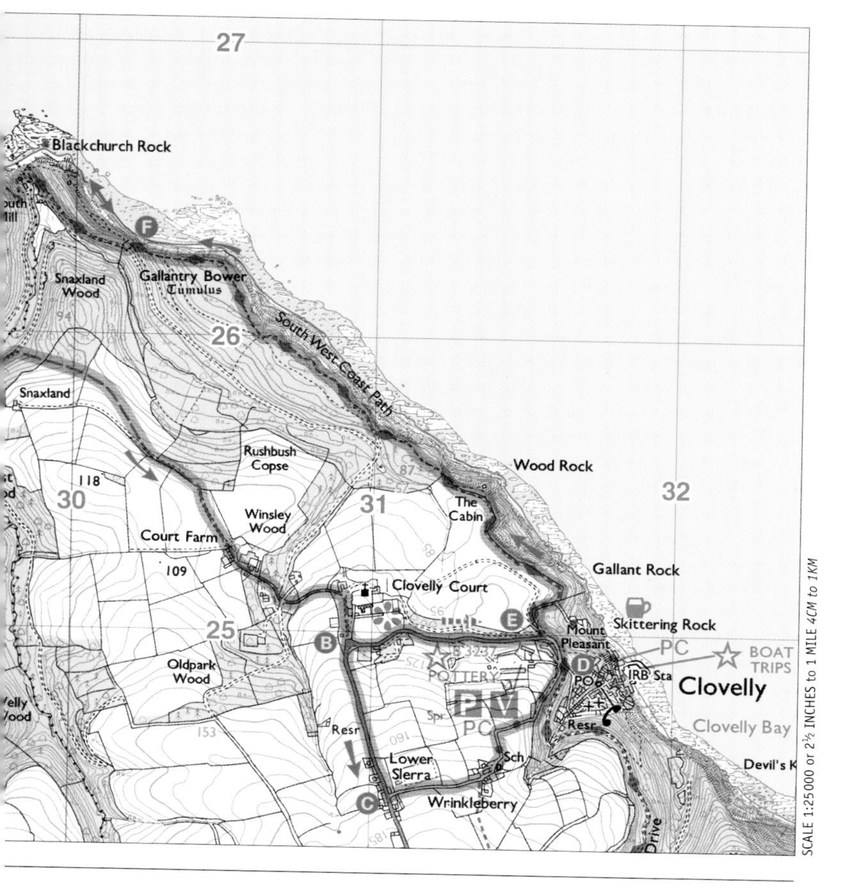

views over Clovelly Bay. The lane descends; where it bears left uphill drop down right through a small parking area. Cross the next lane and go through a gate into parkland E.

The Coast Path soon forks right along the right edge of parkland, then passes through a kissing-gate into rhododendrons to find The Cabin (shelter), built by Sir James Hamlyn Williams in the early 19th century. A kissing-gate leads back into parkland with views of Clovelly Court; the next gate returns to woodland. At the next path junction (church left) bear right on the Coast Path, then right again at the next to reach the Angels Wings, placed there in 1826 by Sir James.

At the next track junction follow the Coast Path right, soon passing through a kissing-gate onto the open ground of Gallantry Bower. A kissing-gate leads back into woodland; descend steeply to a Coast Path post and turn right. Almost immediately reach a path junction; turn right F (leaving the Coast Path) for a short worthwhile detour onto The Wilderness and Lookout Point. The beautiful restored summerhouse overlooking Mouthmill Beach was built by Dame Diana Hamlyn in 1820.

Return to F; keep ahead downhill, soon turning right and descending towards Mouthmill Cove. At the wall above the beach turn left; descend a narrow rocky path to cross the beach, then follow a grassy track inland past a disused limekiln. About 50 yds later turn right on the Coast Path and zigzag steeply uphill (part stepped) through woodland onto Brownsham Cliff, crossing a stile at the top. Bear right along the edge of the field; cross a stile and keep along the right edge of the next, with views towards Lundy. At the end of the field cross a stile; turn left G to leave the Coast Path, soon crossing a V-stile into a field. At the end pass through an open gateway; keep along the right edge of the next. Cross a V-stile into Brownsham Wood, and descend to a junction: keep straight on. The path ascends gradually, eventually bearing left through a gate to return to the car park. ●

View to Windbury Point from the summerhouse

Berrynarbor & Widmouth Head

Start	Berrynarbor
Distance	7 miles (11.1km)
Height gain	1,265 feet (385m)
Approximate time	3½ hours
Parking	Free parking at Berrynarbor community shop; ¾ mile off A399 between Ilfracombe and Combe Martin
Route terrain	Hilly fields and tracks, undulating Coast Path, quiet lanes
Dog friendly	To be kept on leads through fields; non-dog friendly stiles
Ordnance Survey maps	Landranger 180 (Barnstaple & Ilfracombe), Explorers 139 (Bideford, Ilfracombe & Barnstaple) or OL9 (Exmoor)

GPS waypoints

Start	SS 561 466
A	SS 553 458
B	SS 545 461
C	SS 534 466
D	SS 535 476
E	SS 557 480
F	SS 561 478

Delightful Berrynarbor – a frequent best-kept village winner – sits in hilly country a mile from the coast near Ilfracombe. A climb out of the pretty Sterridge Valley and a gentle descent into Hele is followed by one of the least strenuous – but lovely – stretches of North Devon's coastal footpath: just one lengthy stepped up and down to encounter.

From the car park turn left, then left at the junction opposite St Peter's Church; take the first lane left, soon passing the school. Pass the junction at 'Turn Round' and continue downhill; where a footpath goes right, take a raised path on the left through a gate, then a meadow, and another gate to rejoin the lane. Keep ahead over Rock Hill into the Sterridge Valley. The maker of Berrynarbor's famous flowerpot men (seen all over the village) lives at Hillside Cottage, soon passed.

Where the lane bears sharp left (Lower Farm Rows left) bear right through a kissing-gate on a footpath **A**. Climb steadily, then follow the top left edge of a big field. At the end pass a willow clump; do not follow the obvious path, but bear slightly right along the left edge of the next field. At the end cross a stile into a wood. Cross two small streams, then a footbridge/ stile into a field; turn left along the bottom edge. Where the fence bears away keep straight ahead uphill, cutting off the corner. At the top cross a stile, and bear diagonally right across the field: as you crest the top aim for a footpath post in the far hedge. Cross two stiles onto a lane opposite the entrance to Lower Trayne Farm **B**.

Follow the drive downhill. The path is well signed through farm buildings: cross the yard and through a gate to the right of stables. Keep ahead through another gate; turn left through another and follow the track, bearing right downhill into the valley. Pass through a gate and keep ahead, dropping gently to the bottom left corner by Comyn Wood. A gate leads to a woodland path (muddy). Reach Comyn Farm and cross the stream (no footbridge): bear left through a gate between houses, then bear right to a junction.

Turn right Ⓒ, almost immediately turning left through a gate on a narrow hedged path (Cat Lane), eventually meeting a track via a gate on a bend. Keep ahead, gently downhill, to a T-junction with houses opposite. Turn right to meet a narrow lane on a bend; turn right. Just round the bend turn left (signs for the Old Cornmill). Go through the gates and pass between the mill and tearoom. The path eventually meets the road at Hele Ⓓ.

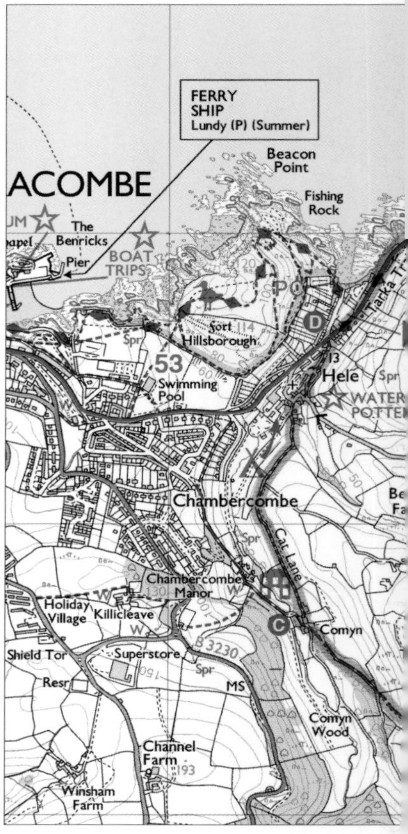

Cross the road with care; turn right. After about ¼ mile bear left on the Coast Path onto Hagginton Point: cross the parking area and continue for 150 yds up the roadside verge; the path then runs parallel to the road, behind a hedge. Bear left at the next Coast Path post, eventually reaching coastguard cottages; turn left to walk around Rillage Point. Cross a stile in woodland at the back of Samson's Bay; emerge from the trees and continue to cross a stile; turn left and walk uphill on a narrow path towards the sea. Descend then climb a long flight of steps onto Widmouth Head. Descend another long flight, and enjoy views along the Exmoor coast. Pass the entrance to Widmouth Farm and cross a stile; continue up a fenced path. Turn left at the top on a wooded path that descends gently. *For about an hour either side of very high tide the foreshore at Water Mouth is*

Water Mouth viewed from the Coast Path

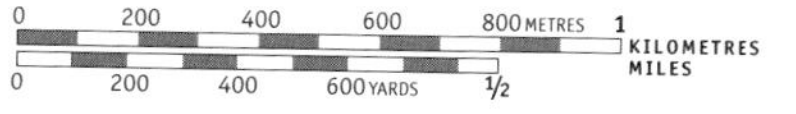

impassable: if so turn right onto the road where indicated, and follow it downhill. The Coast Path descends to the foreshore. Turn right, soon bearing left beneath the harbour wall; turn right to leave the beach and go through a gate *(high water route rejoins)*. Follow the Coast Path left along the verge.

About 50 yds later turn left on a path that parallels the road. Re-emerge on the road at the harbour entrance; 50 yds later turn left E to leave the road again and pass through a gate into Watermouth Valley Camping Park. Keep ahead, meeting a driveway on a bend; bear left uphill. Where the drive ends keep straight on to exit the camping area by a Coast Path post. The path climbs steeply above Broad Strand to meet a track through a gate; turn right, leaving the Coast Path F *(for a visit to the beach turn left and descend 227 steps!)*. Walk down the lane to the A399. Turn right briefly; cross over and take the lane to Berrynarbor, eventually climbing steeply to pass the **Old Globe** and church; go right for the car park. ●

Arlington Court & Loxhore

Start	Arlington Court
Distance	7 miles (11.3km)
Height gain	1,065 feet (325m)
Approximate time	3½ hours
Parking	NT car park at Arlington Court (free); Arlington Court is 5½ miles northeast of Barnstaple, signed off both the A39 and A399
Route terrain	Woodland, parkland, undulating lanes and hedged tracks
Dog friendly	To be kept on leads through the estate and in farmland
Ordnance Survey maps	Landranger 180 (Barnstaple & Ilfracombe), Explorer OL9 (Exmoor)

GPS waypoints

- Start: SS 611 407
- A: SS 614 404
- B: SS 606 398
- C: SS 608 395
- D: SS 600 378
- E: SS 607 375
- F: SS 609 377
- G: SS 617 383
- H: SS 616 387

The 3,500-acre Arlington Court estate, owned by the Chichester family since 1384, was given to the National Trust by Rosalie Chichester two years before her death in 1949. This undulating route explores wooded valleys and parkland and the Yeo Valley, utilising quiet lanes and hedged tracks to reach the hamlet of Loxhore with its 15th-century church.

From the car park turn left. After 300 yds turn right on a lane, which reduces to a track and bears left to a junction A; turn right. Bear right past the stableyard (built in the 1860s; now housing the Carriage Museum) on a gravelled path to reach the church (right); bear left on another gravelled

In the stableyard

path (Arlington Court, built in 1822 in neo-classical style, lies ahead); a few yards on bear left on a narrower path with a lake below left. Pass the lake and descend into woodland. Eventually meet a fork (Wilderness) and keep left, downhill, passing through a gate into parkland. Keep ahead, bearing left through a gate across the Yeo (which meets the Taw at Barnstaple) on Smallacombe Bridge to a path junction.

Turn left **B** on the main track, which follows the river round a right-hand bend to a path junction at Tucker's Bridge (look for the footpath post to the right of the track); take the right fork **C**, signed Shirwell. Pass through a gate on a rough path, which at last rises through a gate, then crosses a stile into

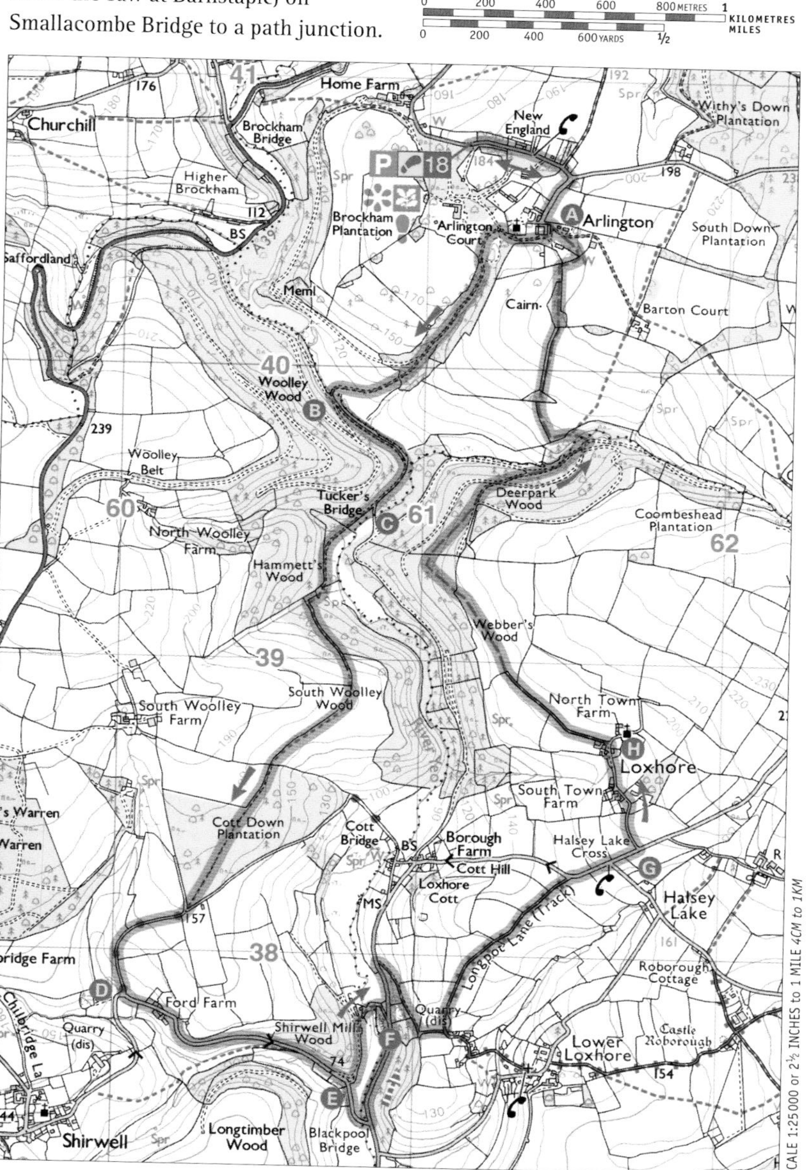

St Michael and All Angels, Loxhore

open country. Turn left; climb steadily above South Woolley Wood, then keep along the left edge of a field. At the corner turn left over a stile (Pynes Hill), then turn right along the top edge of the next field, with lovely views over the Yeo Valley. Cross a stile in the top right corner and follow the narrow path through Cott Down Plantation. Cross a stile at the end onto a track; turn left for a few yards to meet another opposite Cott Down Farm. Turn right downhill on a rough hedged track to meet a lane at Ford Cross.

Turn left **D**. Climb past Ford Farm, then climb a little farther above the Yeo Valley, before descending. When Blackpool Bridge comes into view turn left **E** towards Shirwell Mill. *If you would prefer to avoid a right of way through a garden, keep ahead over Blackpool Bridge, then turn left to rejoin the main route* **F**. Pass through a gate and by the house, at the yard entrance, turn right through a gate across the garden, crossing the river via a gate/footbridge. Keep the hedgebank on the left, bearing right to meet the road again.

Turn left **F**. About 200 yds later turn sharp right through a gate and climb steadily up the right edge of a field, bearing sharp left towards the top to pass through a gate onto a hedged track. Turn left through another gate, and follow the high-hedged track (Longpot Lane) steadily uphill (muddy in winter) eventually to pass through another gate and on to meet the lane.

Turn right; pass Halsey Lake Cross and take the next lane left to Loxhore church **G**. Pass through the pretty hamlet; just before the lane bears right towards the Church of St Michael and All Angels turn left **H** on a bridlepath through a gate, soon passing through another. Follow the wide hedged track to enter a big field via a gate. Keep along the left edge; after 100 yds, where the hedge bears away 90 degrees left, keep straight ahead on a beaten grassy path towards Webber's Wood.

Pass through a gate and follow the woodland path gently downhill, eventually dropping more steeply to a junction; keep straight on, signed Arlington, on a broad level track. At the next junction (Deerpark) keep straight on. The path bears left over a stream, then climbs through a gate. Follow the fenced path ahead, turning right at the field end. The path climbs gently uphill to pass through a strip of woodland, and continues, fenced, with a field right. Pass through an open gate into another strip of woodland – views to Arlington Court across the fields left – and follow the fenced path gently downhill through another gate into a field; turn right along the left edge, soon turning left through a gate into woodland. The path reaches a junction; turn left to meet the footpath post **A**. *For refreshments turn left and make your way to* **Arlington House** *(no entrance charge to café);* otherwise keep ahead and retrace your steps to the car park. ●

Baggy Point & Saunton Down

Start	Croyde
Distance	7¼ miles (11.4km)
Height gain	1,065 feet (325m)
Approximate time	3½ hours
Parking	Pay and Display village hall car park in centre; Croyde is 5 miles northwest of Braunton (via B3231)
Route terrain	Farm tracks, level Coast Path, beach, steep ascent of Saunton Down
Dog friendly	To be kept on leads through fields
Ordnance Survey maps	Landranger 180 (Barnstaple & Ilfracombe), Explorer 139 (Bideford, Ilfracombe & Barnstaple)

GPS waypoints

Start	SS 444 392
A	SS 438 404
B	SS 438 407
C	SS 420 405
D	SS 436 395
E	SS 434 387
F	SS 433 384
G	SS 447 378
H	SS 447 380

The surfing hotspot of Croyde Sand is flanked by the craggy headland of Baggy Point, where two ancient bands of rock meet, and lofty Saunton Down. The Coast Path is not too strenuous here; the trudge along the beach can be tiring and the one steep climb onto Saunton Down is rewarded with beautiful views over Croyde Bay.

From the car park entrance turn left (toilets) and walk steadily up Jones's Hill, passing a left turn to the beach. Where the lane bears sharp right keep ahead on a lane, which reduces to a track and passes Cherry Tree Farm. Keep ahead up the green lane (Broadaway Lane), which is often muddy. Ascend steadily; where the track appears to fork through a gate keep right, eventually bearing sharp left (footpath right).

After 50 yds turn right **A** over a stile. Walk up the left edge of the field; cross a stile, and continue in the same direction, rising gently, with increasingly good views left to Baggy Point and ahead across Morte Bay. Keep ahead to a Coast Path post.

Turn left **B**, soon crossing a stile. The Coast Path runs gently through a series of fields as it wends its way towards Baggy Point. Much of the headland is an SSSI on account of its geological features: raised beaches, onshore platforms and erratic boulders. Cross another stile; eventually pass through a gate into open ground, soon passing a footpath junction. Keep ahead through a gate, with a big slate hedgebank left. The wall eventually bears away sharp left: just round the corner bear right on a broad path to pass the rocket pole (once common around the coast, rockets were launched from such poles in life-saving training). A few yards on keep right at the next path 'junction' to walk along the cliff edge (wire fence right). Keep along the fence, then descend to a gate and turn right through it **C**.

The path drops steeply, then bears sharp left (straight ahead lies The Promontory – keep an eye out for climbers). The Coast Path, now broad and level, runs towards houses; pass through a gate and by an inscription to the writer Henry Williamson who lived locally. The path meets a lane just past Baggy House: note the huge chunk of whalebone, washed up here in 1915. Follow the lane between stone gateposts and houses, and past the NT car park and **Sandleigh Tearoom**. The lane kinks left then right; take a parallel path behind the right hedgebank; where that ends keep along the pavement for 50 yds.

At a Coast Path (toilets) sign turn right **D** and walk towards beachside buildings, with the dunes beyond. *For a shorter walk continue up the lane to reach the T-junction; turn right down Jones's Hill to the car park.* The lane bears right and heads towards the beach. Hit the beach; turn left along the base of the dunes, eventually bear right inland to cross a stream on a bridge, and continue by the dunes again (at low tide it may be easier to walk on harder

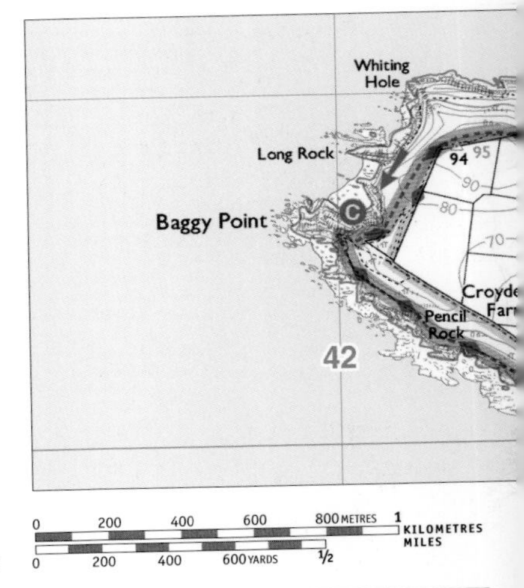

sand nearer the sea, and wade across the stream). At the end of the beach bear right and ascend a ramp onto low rocks. Cross the back of another small beach, then ascend steps.

At the top turn left (toilets ahead) through a kissing-gate **E** on the Coast Path (joined by the Tarka Trail) along a stretch of low cliffs at Downend. Pass through a kissing-gate; very soon after turn sharp left as signed and ascend steeply through a wall gap; ascend steps with a small lookout (left) to reach the road. Turn left.

After 100 yds turn right **F** up steps on the Coast Path. Now follows a lovely long, level section parallel to and high above the road, with stunning views over Saunton Sands and Braunton Burrows *(Walk 9)*. Past Saunton Sands Hotel the path descends to a junction (**Sands Café**: *turn right across the road, and descend to the beach)*.

Turn left **G** over a stile ('alternative coast path') and climb very steeply up a narrow woodland path, stepped in places, with a stream right. The path bears left away from the stream and climbs to cross a stile into a field. Keep ahead to a footpath post **H** (alternative Coast Path right to pass ruined Down Cottage).

Croyde Sand from the Coast Path

Keep ahead up the field to find a footpath post by a gate at the top. Pass through; keep ahead up the left edge of a meadow, with a low hedgebank left, over the top of Saunton Down. Cross a stile/metal gate, and keep ahead to a double stile at the end of the field. Pause to enjoy wonderful views over Croyde and Baggy Point. Bear right past a footpath post, and keep ahead to the next one: bear right, along the contours, to cross a stile into woodland, almost immediately crossing another. Continue on a narrow downhill path (parts muddy). Reach a footpath junction and keep ahead through a kissing-gate, then along a narrow hedged path. Pass through another kissing-gate and later a five-bar gate onto a concrete way: turn left down Cloutman's Lane. The lane becomes metalled on reaching houses; keep ahead to Croyde Road, near **The Thatch** and **Billy Budds** (pubs); turn right, soon turning left into the car park. ●

Trentishoe Down & Heddon's Mouth Cleave

Start	Heddon's Gate
Distance	6¾ miles (10.8km)
Height gain	1,490 feet (455m)
Approximate time	4 hours
Parking	NT car park (honesty box) and laneside parking at Heddon's Gate, signed off A399 between Blackmoor Gate and Combe Martin
Route terrain	Woodland tracks, moorland, uneven Coast Path, long and steep descent to finish
Dog friendly	To be kept on leads on Coast Path (sheep)
Ordnance Survey maps	Landranger 180 (Barnstaple & Ilfracombe), Explorer OL9 (Exmoor)

GPS waypoints

Start	SS 655 481
A	SS 638 475
B	SS 635 469
C	SS 625 476
D	SS 627 478
E	SS 649 491
F	SS 652 482

Heddon's Mouth is one of Exmoor's few accessible coves, the haunt of smugglers in the 18th and 19th centuries. Although just a short stroll along the valley from Heddon's Gate, it's best appreciated from the Coast Path, which runs high above. This walk crosses lofty Trentishoe Down and follows the spectacular coast before encountering the sessile oak woodlands of the Heddon Valley.

Walk towards **The Hunters Inn** – the original thatched inn, popular in Victorian times with students from Oxford and Cambridge universities on walking tours, burned down in 1895 (see later) – passing to its left on Josey's Lane, soon crossing the Heddon River. Just before the next bridge over the Blackmoor Water turn left through a gate on a bridlepath/permitted path. Reach a junction of footpaths and turn right to pass to the left of a pretty cottage and cross a stream to meet another path. Turn left along the level track through woodland; at a fork follow the lower (left) path, which descends alongside an old wall to meet

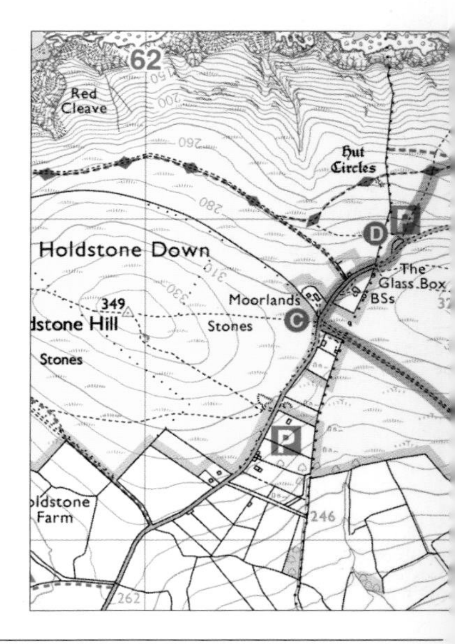

a lane; turn left.

After a few yards turn right as signed on a rocky footpath (signed Ladies Mile). Climb very steeply through woodland to a footpath junction on the edge of Trentishoe Down. Turn left Ⓐ on Ladies Mile, a lovely narrow path along the top edge of woodland. The path eventually leads to Trentishoe Manor, at one time the rectory; it is said that the Ladies Mile was constructed so that the ladies of the manor could walk to church at Trentishoe (see later). Where you spot a lane below left, look for a narrow path bearing off right uphill and turn right Ⓑ, leaving Ladies Mile. It's a pretty steady uphill climb, with the occasional short level stretch. Eventually rise above the woodland into bracken and gorse on a broad grassy path, parallel to a drystone wall left; where the wall bears away 90 degrees left, keep straight ahead uphill, passing to the right of a big stand of gorse. Meet a rough track by a small post and keep ahead uphill. Follow the track over the edge of Trentishoe Down, home to a group of Bronze Age barrows; it levels off to meet a road, to the left of The Glass House, an unusual contemporary building with huge windows. Just to the west can be seen the swell of Holdstone Down, the highest coastal hill in the southwest, rising to 1,145ft above Exmoor's famous rugged hog's-back cliffs.

Turn right Ⓒ and walk along the

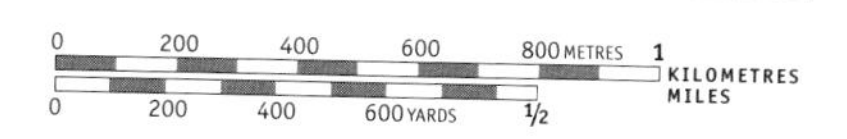

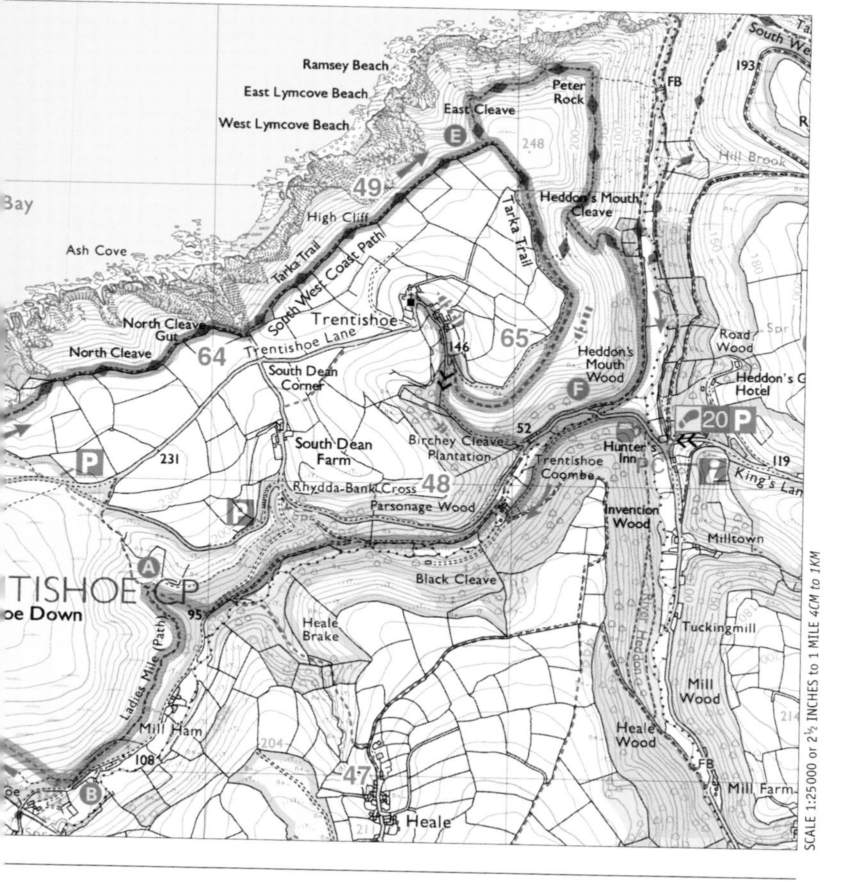

lane, descending gently, with fabulous views towards the cliffs on the east side of Heddon's Mouth and The Beacon *(Walk 15)*. At the first parking area on the left (the lane ahead descends and bears right), bear left **D** through it to find a broad grassy path which passes two benches and continues downhill to meet the Coast Path.

Lamb on the Coast Path

Turn right and follow the Coast Path downhill (rocky underfoot), with stunning views ahead. At the next fork keep straight on. Pass through a gate and continue across an area of grassland, to pass through another gate above Neck Wood. Continue alongside a bank, soon passing through a gate to clip the edge of a field; then through another.

Keep ahead, eventually to meet a footpath post and follow the Coast Path left **E**. *For an alternative finish – and if you want to visit St Peter's Church at Trentishoe – turn right here along a glorious path which runs high above the Heddon Valley to meet the lane just below the church; turn right uphill. There are records of a church here as long ago as 1260, and it's well worth a visit for its squat, castellated tower and 18th-century minstrel's gallery; there are rumours that smugglers' contraband was at one time hidden in the tower. To finish follow the lane downhill into Trentishoe Combe, turning left on meeting the lane to rejoin the route at* **F**. The Coast Path narrows and becomes quite exposed, and rocky in places, before turning sharp right at Peter Rock above Heddon's Mouth. Down on the rocky beach below is an unusual restored 19th-century double limekiln (*Walk 15*). The path runs inland up the Heddon Valley, later dropping across an area of scree (the result of intense freeze–thaw activity on the underlying sandstone during the Ice Age), then zigzags steeply downhill to enter woodland. Pass through a small gate, and continue downhill to meet a broad track. Turn right and keep ahead along the valley bottom to meet a lane through a kissing-gate.

Turn left **F** to pass Harry's Orchard (stocked with traditional English varieties, and open to the public) and cross the Heddon River to return to your car. The Hunter's Inn was bought by Benjamin Green Lake *(Walk 15)* in 1885; by summer 1895 Lake had constructed the carriage drive from here to Woody Bay. After the disastrous fire the hotel was rebuilt in Swiss chalet style in 1897, and continues to flourish to this day.

Chulmleigh & Eggesford Forest

Start	Chulmleigh
Distance	7½ miles (12.1km)
Height gain	1,115 feet (340m)
Approximate time	4 hours
Parking	Free parking in New Street by St Mary Magdalene Church, off the A377 between Barnstaple and Copplestone
Route terrain	Undulating route: farmland, woodland tracks, rural lanes
Dog friendly	Dogs to be kept on leads through farmland
Ordnance Survey maps	Landranger 180 (Barnstaple & Ilfracombe), Explorer 127 (South Molton & Chulmleigh)

GPS waypoints

- Start: SS 686 141
- A: SS 688 141
- B: SS 697 138
- C: SS 704 128
- D: SS 711 125
- E: SS 695 110
- F: SS 688 114
- G: SS 684 129

Chulmleigh, once on an important north–south coaching route, was a centre of the woollen industry until the late 17th century. This attractive little town sits on a hill above the valleys of the Little Dart and Taw, the ideal starting point for this lengthy route (with a steep finish) through peaceful and undulating farmland, woods and valleys.

Retrace your steps to the village centre opposite the **Red Lion Hotel**, and turn right. Where the road bears sharp right and descends turn left **A** (The Old Rectory right) along an unnamed lane. Pass the cricket club, and follow the lane downhill.

In the valley bottom cross a bridge to pass Park Mill; as the lane bears sharp left keep ahead over a stile **B**. Follow the right field edge: the old mill leat lies through trees to the right. Near the field end turn right over a stile and drop to cross two footbridges and a stile. Bear left along the edge of a big water meadow – the Little Dart River runs along the far side. Pass through a hedge gap and continue along the left edge of the next meadow (damp underfoot).

When level with a big footbridge turn right and cross the river: follow footpath posts to twist through a conifer plantation (muddy), eventually bearing left uphill to meet a woodland track (bluebells in spring). Bear left uphill. At the top leave the woodland to bear right along the right edge of a field, heading towards portacabins; just before reaching them turn left and walk up the right hedge. At the top pass through an open gateway; bear diagonally left across the corner of the next field to meet a fence and turn right. At the field end bear left through a gate onto a lane.

Turn left **C** to pass Hollow Tree Cross and continue through Chawleigh. About

50 yds beyond **The Royal Oak Inn** (opposite 'Toilets'), turn right **D** down a track, which becomes a green lane, uneven underfoot, with a boggy section after wet weather. *To avoid this continue along the road, turn right at the first junction, and rejoin the route at Tatworthy Farm.* The lane reaches a gate into a field: keep along the right edge to pass through another. Turn left; follow the fence towards Tatworthy Farm. At the field top bear right through a metal gate; pass through several farmyard gates to reach the lane. Turn right on the Little Dart Ridge and Valley Walk, which has a spur to Chulmleigh. The lane reaches a fork at Southcott Cross, with views of Dartmoor's northern tors.

Pass through the gate mid-fork and straight across the field. Climb a stile; bear slightly left along the edge of the next field to pass through a gate onto a lane. Turn left. The lane kinks right; as it kinks left bear right through a gate into a field. Bear left; keep ahead towards buildings. At the farmyard wall

Green lane near Chawleigh

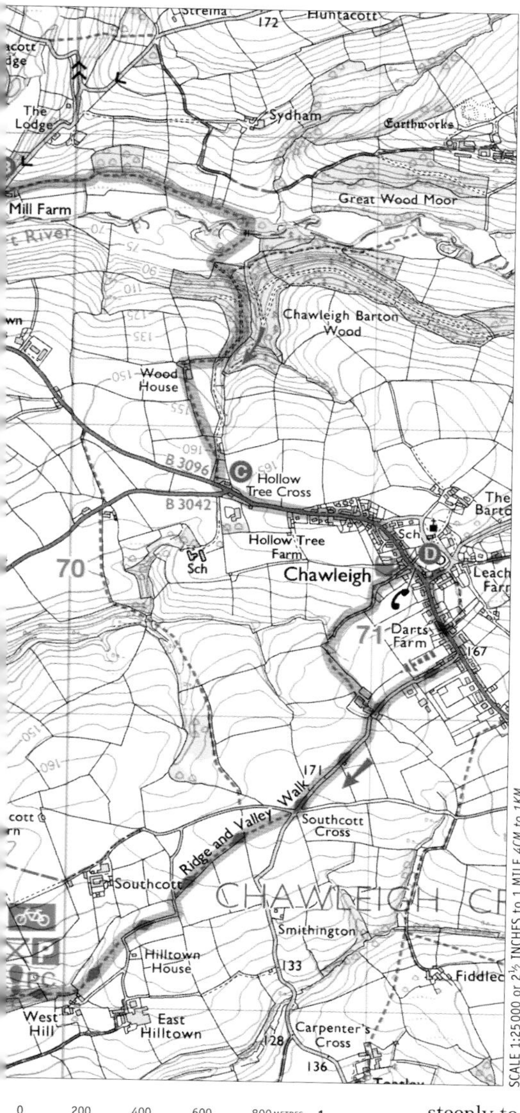

0 200 400 600 800 METRES 1 KILOMETRES
0 200 400 600 YARDS ½ MILES

turn right over a stile; follow the narrow path into a field, bearing left along the top edge. Pass through a gate into another, which drops steeply right. Bear half right, descending gradually towards the valley-bottom stream, which you cross near the field end. Pass through a gate onto a track and footpath junction in Eggesford Forest.

Turn right **E**; almost immediately bear right off the main track and climb steeply, bearing right towards the top of the wood, levelling off before bearing left to a path junction. Turn left on a broad bridleway and walk steadily downhill, with views across the Taw Valley to Eggesford church. Pass through a parking area to meet the A377.

A few yards later, before cottages, turn right **F**. Cross a stile into a field and walk along the bottom right edge. Pass below a stand of gorse; follow a broad path uphill and through a gate to the left of buildings at Nethercott. Turn right, then left at the field end to reach a lane. Turn right; after 100 yds turn left to descend through woodland. Cross a stile, then follow a broad track through Upcott Wood. Where it bears sharp right keep ahead over a stile/ footbridge into a field. Walk diagonally (slightly left) across, aiming for a gate onto a lane in the far corner.

Turn right **G**; climb steeply to Chawleigh Week Cross. Keep ahead (unsuitable for cars); as the lane bears right bear left (dead end). The lane reduces to a track to buildings at Chawleigh Week; just past the farmhouse, as the main track bears left, bear right, dropping steeply to cross the Little Dart via a footbridge. The track (Rock Hill – an ancient trackway to Copplestone) climbs very steeply to reach Chulmleigh, with the church wall ahead. Turn left for your car.

Morte Point

		GPS waypoints
Start	Mortehoe	SS 457 452
Distance	7½ miles (12km)	A SS 465 455
Height gain	1,885 feet (575m)	B SS 472 456
Approximate time	4 hours	C SS 482 452
Parking	Car park at Mortehoe (Pay and Display): Mortehoe is signed off B3343 (off A361 at Mullacott Cross between Braunton and Ilfracombe)	D SS 483 463 E SS 479 464 F SS 475 467 G SS 462 467 H SS 453 449
Route terrain	Farmland, wooded valley, Coast Path (steep ascents/descents)	
Ordnance Survey maps	Landranger 180 (Barnstaple & Ilfracombe), Explorer 139 (Bideford, Ilfracombe & Barnstaple)	

A medieval farmstead, rolling unimproved grassland, an ancient wooded valley, a secluded cove, a lighthouse, some of North Devon's oldest and most dangerous rocks off Morte Point, the death of many a ship ... this classic walk has it all. This deservedly popular section of Coast Path enjoys a succession of ascents and descents – and glorious wildflowers in spring.

Take the lane opposite the car park, signed to Lee, to pass North Morte Farm campsite. Where the way ahead is barred by a gate marked 'Bull Point Lighthouse', take the footpath to the right of a gate to the right. Pass through the campsite at Easewell on a tarmac way. Cross a parking area, and follow footpath signs ahead between buildings. Look carefully for a narrow concrete path that drops between the buildings left. Follow this to pass a pond and cross a stile into a field. Bear slightly left then right uphill to pass through a gate at Yarde Farm.

Turn left A, almost immediately crossing a stile. The track bears right, reduces to a hedged path and ascends shallow steps. Cross a stile into a field, and follow the left edge. Pass through a small gate towards the end, drop to cross a stile, and keep along the left

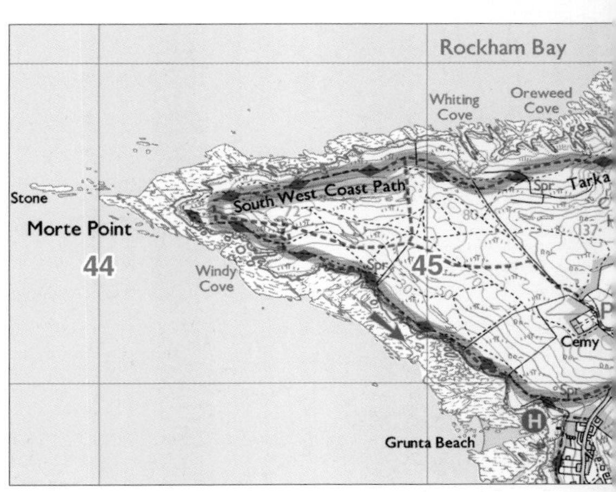

edge of the next. Cross a stile/gate at the end to meet a farm drive on a bend. Bear left; follow the drive towards buildings at atmospheric Damage Barton, dating from the mid-17th century (but there is evidence of a dwelling here in medieval times). Keep a look out for footpath arrows and follow the track past the farmhouse. On reaching a junction of paths turn right Ⓑ, and follow the track slightly uphill, with a wall right. At the T-junction turn left; just before meeting a big gate turn sharp right (unsigned) along a grassy path, bearing left through a gate after about 100 yds. Bear right; walk gently uphill, aiming for a footpath post. Turn right up a broad open track to another post. Keep ahead along the track to pass through a gate and cross a field. Aim for a footpath post on a small hillock ahead; pass to the left of it (with hedgebank left) to meet a small gate. Go through the gate, then bear half-right across the next field, aiming for a footpath post/stile onto a lane.

Cross the lane and stile into a field, then bear slightly right, soon crossing a stile into Borough Wood. Descend steeply under beech trees to a T-junction; turn left Ⓒ, almost immediately crossing a stile, and follow the path gently downhill for 3/4 mile (muddy in parts). At the bottom of the wood meet a path junction and turn right over a footbridge/stile; cross the field and stile onto a narrow path (**The Grampus Inn** is a short detour right).

Turn left Ⓓ; follow the path to join a narrow tarmac lane, which meets the lane and sea wall at Lee Bay. Known locally as 'Fuchsia Valley' for its wealth of wildflowers, Lee has some lovely 16th/17th cottages, but was notorious for smuggling in the 18th and 19th

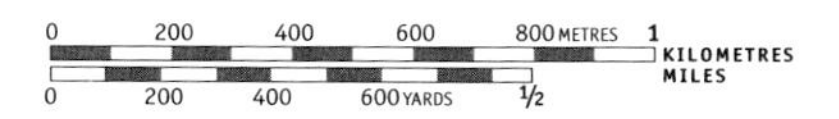

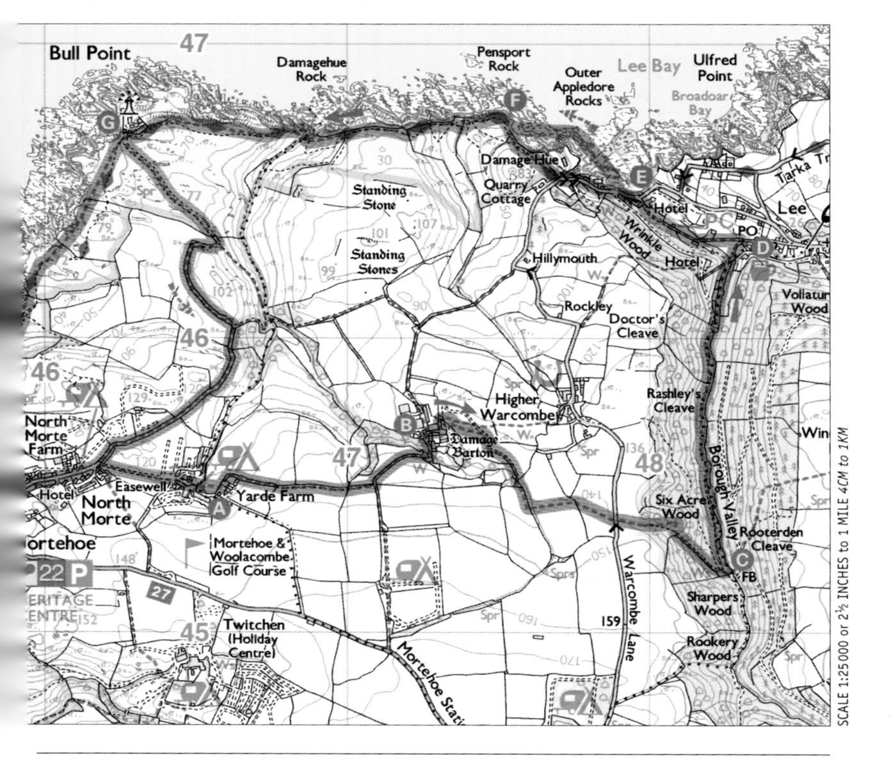

Sandy Cove, with Lee Bay beyond

centuries. Turn left Ⓔ to pass the café at **Smugglers Cottage**. *Note that there is an alternative low-tide route: follow a concrete walkway across the beach, aiming for a cleft in the rocks on the left-hand side: follow the path carefully through the rocks (steps cut in places) to reach Sandy Cove. Walk across and up steep steps to rejoin the route* Ⓕ. The lane climbs very steeply past splendid houses; turn right on the Coast Path through a gate. The path descends steps to meet the alternative from Sandy Cove Ⓕ.

Now follows a delightful section of Coast Path, with a succession of ascents and descents, but none very long. Drop into a combe to cross a footbridge, then zigzag up the other side through gorse. A level section ends at a stile and a steep descent into the next combe, with wonderful views (note that parts of the path are quite badly eroded). Cross a stream on a footbridge, then a stile, and zigzag uphill again.

A lovely level stretch across downland follows; pass Bull Point, then descend to pass to the left of the lighthouse wall (built 1879, demanned in 1995) and reach the entrance Ⓖ. *For a shortcut turn left here and follow the road for 1 mile back to Mortehoe.* Keep ahead up steps and continue on the Coast Path, soon negotiating another combe and a long stepped ascent. Pass a post at Windy Lag then descend to Rockham Bay (access to beach). Cross a stile/gate behind the beach, then ascend steps. At the next stile Mortehoe is signed left; keep ahead. Pass another footpath to Mortehoe and cross a stile, and ascend a long flight of steps. Enjoy views to Lundy *(Walk 24)* and the turbulent waters off Morte Point around the Morte Stone; keep an eye out for grey seals in summer, which return to Lundy in winter to breed. Eventually rocky Morte Point – a jagged confusion of saw-toothed Morte Slates – is reached, carpeted with pink thrift in early summer.

The Coast Path runs on more smoothly towards the edge of Woolacombe. Follow signs along the cliffs to reach a path junction above Grunta Beach and turn left, signed Mortehoe Ⓗ. Climb steeply uphill to reach the road through a gate; turn left to walk through Mortehoe to the car park.

Buck's Mills & Peppercombe

Start	Parkham
Distance	7½ miles (12km)
Height gain	1,490 feet (455m)
Approximate time	4 hours
Parking	Lay-by on left just south of The Bell Inn and Parkham primary school; Parkham is 2¾ miles from A39, Horns Cross, 7 miles west of Bideford
Route terrain	Rolling farmland, woodland tracks, Coast Path, green lanes
Dog friendly	To be kept on leads through fields
Ordnance Survey maps	Landranger 190 (Bude & Clovelly), Explorer 126 (Clovelly & Hartland)

GPS waypoints

- SS 387 210
- A SS 378 221
- B SS 371 230
- C SS 358 233
- D SS 355 235
- E SS 381 241
- F SS 384 231
- G SS 390 222

Circular Coast Path routes always pose a dilemma: where to start? It's preferable if the coastal section comes in the middle: hence Parkham is the start point for this route, which crosses rolling farmland to meet the coast at the tranquil old fishing hamlet of Buck's Mills, then follows a particularly quiet section of Coast Path through oak woodland to peaceful Peppercombe.

Walk towards the crossroads, with **The Bell Inn** right. Keep ahead on Barton Road. Where the lane bears right turn left to Broad Parkham. Follow the lane between hedgebanks for about 3/4 mile, eventually descending into the River Yeo Valley and a junction at Foxdown Cross: keep straight ahead to cross a bridge by Lillyford Mill, then climb steeply uphill.

On reaching buildings at the edge of Broad Parkham, where the lane starts to curve slightly left, bear right **A** on an unsigned track through farm buildings. The hedged green lane ascends to a junction; keep ahead uphill. Climb steadily to the hilltop, with lovely views, before descending gently (muddy and uneven). Keep right at a fork; continue downhill to meet the A39 **B**.

Cross with care. Walk up the small lane opposite: after 150 yds turn left through a kissing-gate into a field, and walk along the top edge. Pass through a gate at the end; follow the right edge of the next. At the end bear right through a small gate; cross a grassy area to a path junction at Lower Worthygate. Turn left, passing behind the farmhouse. Follow yellow arrows, soon passing through a gate to the left of a large open-fronted barn. Pass around a stile, then walk along the left edge of the next field: ahead lies the Buck's Mills

Valley. Halfway along the field the path leads through a gate into woodland. Follow this – the old Coffin Path to Parkham, used before the consecration of St Anne's at Buck's Mills – downhill, eventually to cross a small stream on a footbridge, then follow the main stream downhill. The path passes between cottages to emerge onto a lane in Buck's Mills C.

Turn right towards the coast. For generations Buck's Mills was a small fishing hamlet with a quay (built in 1598 and long gone) and two limekilns, and a corn-grinding mill: today it's remarkably quiet and unspoilt. The name 'Braund' is prevalent, thought originally to result from seven shipwrecked Spanish brothers (possibly during the time of the Armada) who married local girls; more recent theories put the descendants' Mediterranean looks down to prehistoric Iberian immigrants. A steep path leads to the rocky beach, characterised by contorted folds of siltstone, sandstone and shale.

Look for a Coast Path sign pointing right by the telephone box D. Ascend steps into Worthygate Woods; a long climb eventually leads to a path junction. Follow the Coast Path ahead into open and easier country: a long undulating stretch along Worthygate and Sloo Woods, with good views back to Clovelly. Eventually the path starts to descend into the Peppercombe Valley, passing a small viewpoint near the site of an Iron Age promontory fort. Steps lead to a path junction in the valley bottom, with Peppercombe beach left. Follow Coast Path signs right E to cross a stream: where the Coast Path turns left keep ahead, inland, signed Horns Cross. Where the track meets a U-bend keep right, descending slightly. Follow the narrow banked path to the right of Coastguard Cottages and ascend

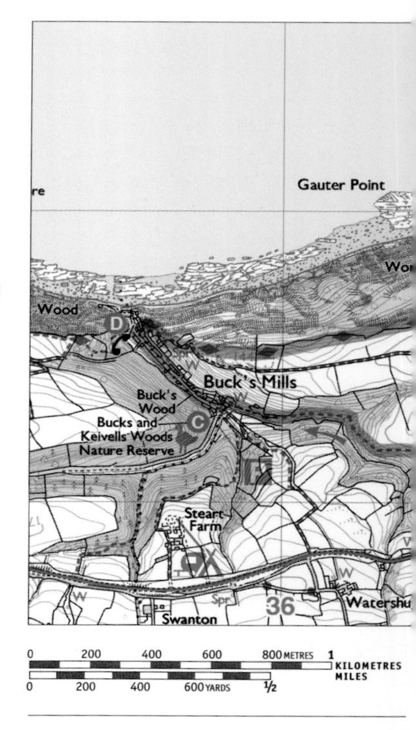

steeply, passing two more, and continue up a steeply ascending track which meets a lane; turn right to the A39 at Horns Cross, by the **Coach & Horses** pub F.

Cross with care, and turn right. After 100 yds turn left on a public footpath, bearing right over a stile into a field. Turn left along the left edge; pass through a gate at the end onto a farm lane on a bend, and keep ahead, downhill, to pass through the yard at West Goldworthy: Parkham church comes into view. Keep straight on past a big open-fronted barn on a hedged green lane, which ends at a gate. Cross a stile to the left as signed, and follow the left edge of the next huge field, with woodland left. Pass through a gate at the end: descend steps and bear right to almost immediately cross a stile. Keep ahead, gently downhill, along the right edge of the next field, bearing right through a metal gate, with a white cottage left, to a footpath junction: turn

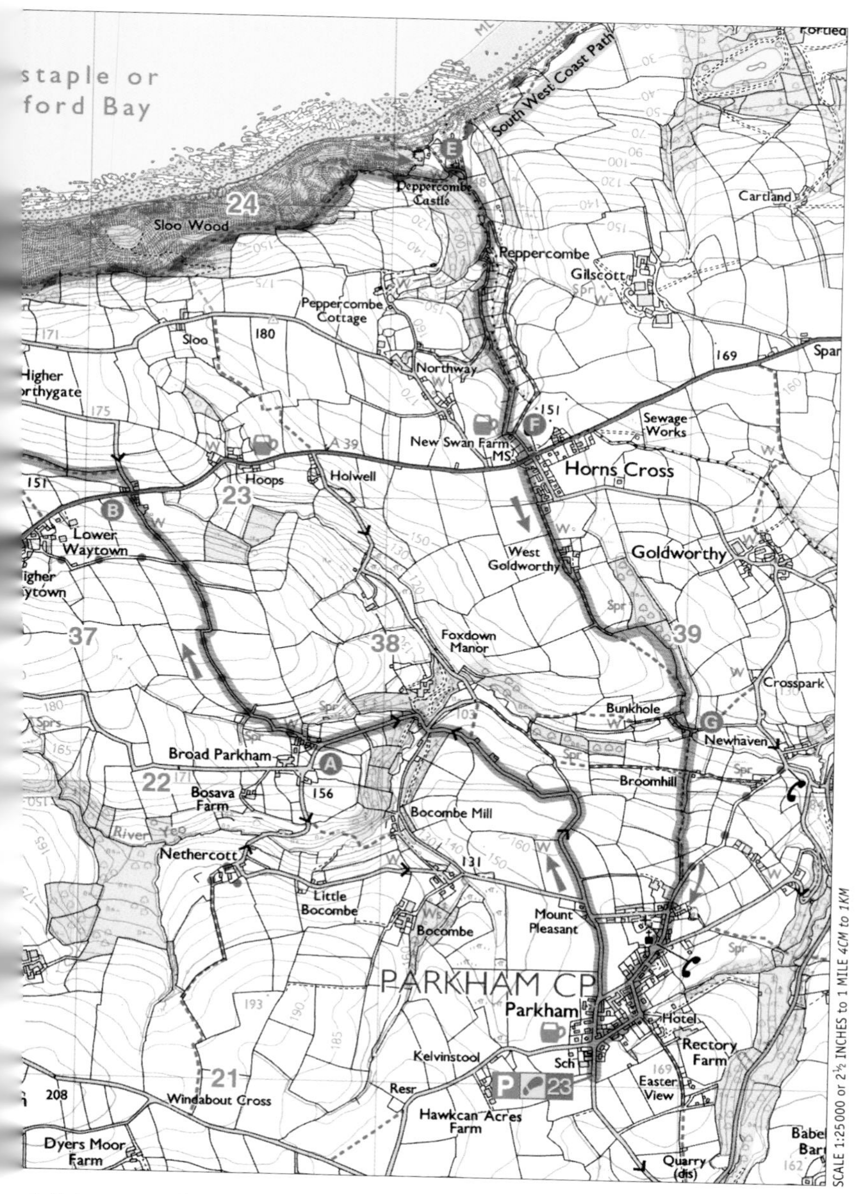

left down a track. At the next footpath post turn right G over a stream on a footbridge.

Keep straight across the next field, aiming for a gate to the right of an open-fronted barn. Pass through; ascend the left edge of the next field, climbing steps to cross a stile at the top. Keep straight ahead across the next field, eventually keeping left of a hedge to reach a gate onto a green lane: turn right to find Hill View Farm at the edge of Parkham. Reach a lane on a corner; keep ahead to pass the 15th-century Church of St James. Turn left down Rectory Lane, soon bearing right. At the end of the lane by The Bell Inn turn left to your car.

Lundy Island

Start	Marisco Tavern
Distance	8 miles (12.5km). Short option 3¾ miles (6km)
Height gain	1,310 feet (400m). Short option 950 feet (290m)
Approximate time	4 hours. Short option 1½ hours
Access	Contact the Shore Office (see Useful Organisations). The *MS Oldenburg* sails from Ilfracombe or Bideford March–November (not daily); winter helicopter service from Hartland Point
Route terrain	Narrow rocky cliff paths, moorland, grassland; unsuitable for those suffering from vertigo
Dog friendly	Dogs not permitted on Lundy
Ordnance Survey maps	Landranger 180 (Barnstaple & Ilfracombe), Explorer 139 (Bideford, Ilfracombe & Barnstaple)

GPS waypoints

Start	SS 137 440
A	SS 140 440
B	SS 138 452
C	SS 138 456
D	SS 132 472
E	SS 130 481
F	SS 130 450
G	SS 132 442
H	SS 134 436
J	SS 141 437

This flat-topped granite island – 3 miles long and ½ mile wide – sits 11½ miles off Hartland Point. There's nothing between Lundy and the USA's east coast, and her 450ft- (137m-) high cliffs receive a battering from Atlantic storms. But it's a magical place, steeped in history, renowned for its flora and fauna and with an irresistible magnetism.

Where you walk on Lundy depends on how long you have – and on the weather! This route assumes reasonable weather (in terms of wind and rain) and a good few hours. On a day trip, your time on Lundy depends on how you get there. The long walk circumnavigates the Island; the shorter option will suit those who have less time. There's a quick 'escape route' via the track to the village (about 75 minutes' walking time, plus 20 to the Landing Beach).

Start from the **Marisco Tavern**. (If coming straight off the boat join at Ⓐ after a steep climb from the Landing Beach.) Turn left past toilets and through a gate. Head across grassland and through a gate, then descend to Millcombe House (completed in 1836 for William Hudson Heaven, who bought Lundy in 1834). Bear left downhill to meet a track on a bend. Bear left to reach a stone building (originally a cowshed) right and pond left.

Turn left Ⓐ through a gate onto a narrow path, with lovely views of the East Sideland. This path once tunnelled through rhododendron, planted in Victorian times, but after an aggressive clearance programme is back in the open. Cross a stile and pass a rare group of trees, flourishing on Lundy's sheltered east side; climb to cross a granite outcrop. Climb to another stile, then pass through the former quarry – during its short life from 1863 almost 300 people worked for the Lundy Granite Company – soon crossing an incline down which granite was lowered to Quarry Beach. Pass a bird trap; a path right descends right to the beach, with old holding bays left.

A narrow path turns sharp left B. *Short route: turn left uphill to pass a small granite building dedicated to Felix Gade, Lundy's agent from 1926 to 1978. Descend steps to a quarry pond; ascend and turn right inland, later keeping left at a fork, to a track by another pond. Turn left for a few paces; strike right across rough ground (boggy), keeping left of gorse, parallel to a wire fence left. Meet the main route at* F. Follow an old tramway track ahead to pass the VC Quarry, home to a Second World War memorial John Pennington Harman, son of Martin Coles Harman, who introduced the Lundy pony to the Island. The path rises and starts to bear inland, with views towards Tibbetts (a former Admiralty lookout) built in 1909 on Lundy's second-highest point.

Just past a huge spoil heap (right), bear right C on a narrow path (by a lump of worked granite)

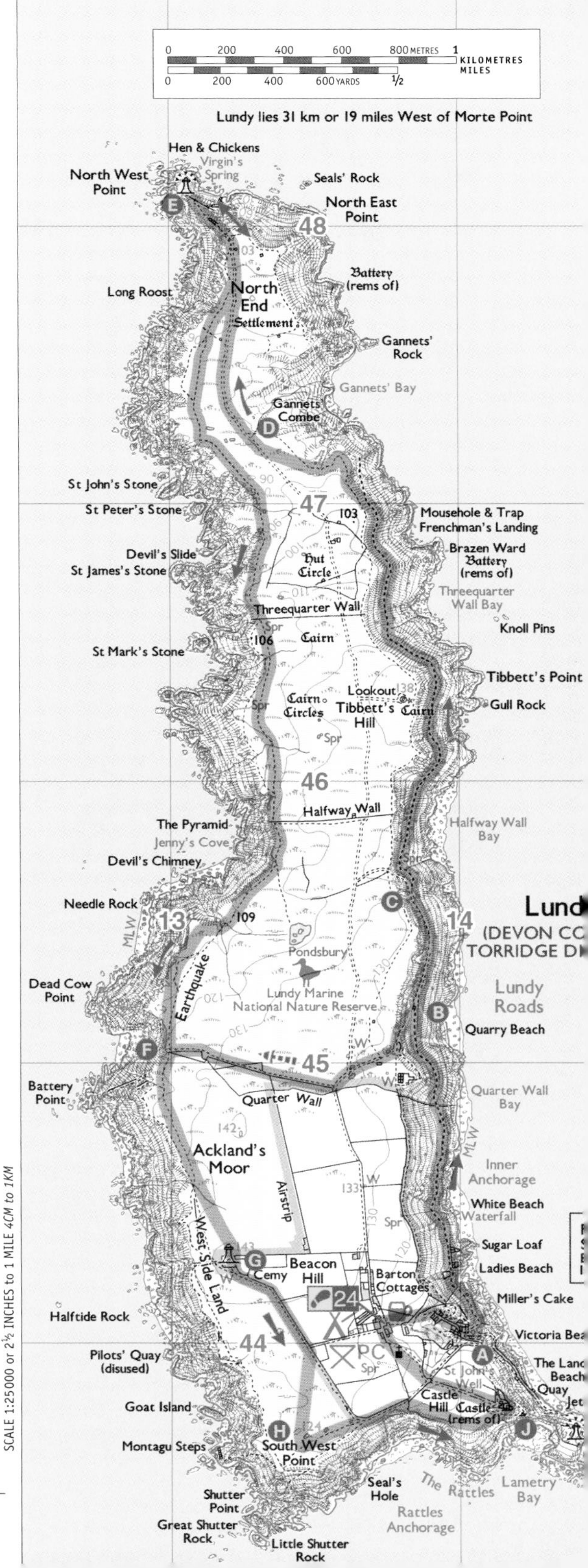

Lundy is home to a breeding colony of around 60 grey seals

that runs below granite stacks. Hardy Soay sheep, introduced in 1944, are often seen here: listen out for oystercatchers. Cross a stile below Threequarter Wall; as the path bears left a tiny path drops steeply to Brazen Ward (a 17th-century coastal fortification). Keep an eye out for Sika deer, introduced in 1927. Round a corner to overlook Gannets' Bay – look out for grey seals. From the viewpoint bear left on a winding narrow path, eventually meeting the track (marked by granite blocks).

Turn right D and walk to the top of the Island. Keep ahead downhill via steps to the North Light E, marking the junction of the Bristol Channel and Atlantic Ocean.

Return to the track, and walk south (you may see feral goats). Cut right to join one of several paths. Ahead granite buttresses cling to the cliffs; keep slightly inland to avoid narrow paths to these. Cross a boggy combe on granite blocks, and Threequarter Wall via a stile. The Cheeses at the end of Halfway Wall come into view. Cross the wall, soon keeping towards the coast to avoid boggy ground. Descend into the wet Punchbowl Valley; cross as best you can. A narrow path runs towards the clifftop to join a bigger one; follow this past chasms, said to be linked to the Lisbon earthquake of 1755. Continue along cliffs, later bearing left to join the path towards Quarter Wall. Cross a stile in a fence F; take the right-hand path ahead to find the top of a granite wall to the Battery, a fog-signalling station built in 1863. Continue towards the Old Light, built in 1819 on the island's highest point, but abandoned when the North and South Lights were built in 1897; cross a stile into the compound to the left of the lighthouse G.

Walk ahead through a gate and downhill past Beacon Hill Cemetery (5th- and 6th-century standing stones). At the third gate in the wall (left) bear right, aiming to for a pole marking the Rocket Pole Pond near the southwest tip H.

Turn left on a broad path, soon with a wall left. Do not go through a gate in the wall ahead, but bear right over a stile. Take the right-hand path to Marisco Castle, built in 1244 J, overlooking the South Light.

Follow the track towards St Helena's Church (built in 1896 by the appropriately named Reverend Heaven, whose family owned Lundy at that time), then take a grassy path to the church. Rejoin the track to the village; turn right for the Tavern.

Dolton, Huish & the River Torridge

Start	Dolton
Distance	8¾ miles (14.1km)
Height gain	1,380 feet (420m)
Approximate time	4½ hours
Parking	The Square, Dolton (free); Dolton is signed off A3124 at Dolton Beacon 5 miles north of Winkleigh
Route terrain	Hilly fields, woodland, parkland, lanes; muddy sections all year round
Dog friendly	To be kept on leads through parkland and farmland
Ordnance Survey maps	Landranger 180 (Barnstaple & Ilfracombe), Explorer 127 (South Molton & Chulmleigh)

GPS waypoints

- (start) SS 570 121
- A SS 566 125
- B SS 558 126
- C SS 555 139
- D SS 543 144
- E SS 544 137
- F SS 530 123
- G SS 533 110
- H SS 547 111
- J SS 550 112

This is an in-depth exploration of remote and undulating countryside around the Torridge Valley. Stretches on narrow lanes are unavoidable, but the only traffic you are likely to meet is the occasional tractor or post van. The walk visits the tiny hamlet of Huish, little more than a church and farm, but home to more than 120 people in the late 19th century.

Dolton is one of Mid Devon's prettiest villages, with a wealth of thatched cottages. St Edmund's Church dates from the 14th century but was mostly rebuilt in the mid-19th, and has an unusual font fashioned from parts of a Saxon cross.

(start) With your back to the **Royal Oak** pub (and bus shelter a few yards to the right) cross the road and follow a footpath between thatched cottages. Where the tarmac way bends right keep ahead through a gate on a gravel drive, then ahead through another into a field. Pass through a gate and continue downhill on a fenced grassy path. Cross a stile and stream at the bottom; follow the path uphill through woodland, soon crossing another stile onto a grassy track. Turn right up the

Cottage at Merton Mill Cross

right edge of a huge field to meet a track via a gate at Iddlecott (a Domesday manor).

Turn left Ⓐ. The track (muddy in places) bears right and continues between high hedges, later bearing left. Where it narrows and starts to drop (large beech tree ahead) bear right through a gate with a footpath arrow and walk diagonally across the field, aiming to the right of the far left corner; Halsdon House, once home to the poet William Cory (1823–92), comes into view ahead. Cross a stile into woodland; keep ahead over a stream and leave the wood over another stile. Head across the next field to a gate; bear right through it, then bear left downhill, aiming to the left of a white cottage across the stream ahead. Cross a very wet patch in the bottom corner; cross the stream via a stile/footbridge to meet a track opposite cottages. Turn left uphill; soon turn right on a narrow deeply banked footpath that climbs steeply to a lane.

Turn right Ⓑ along the lane for almost 1 mile, ascending past Halsdon House and the Devon Wildlife Trust's Halsdon Reserve. Just before the lane bears right at South Harepath turn left Ⓒ through a gate on a track that drops downhill to pass through another, with lovely views across the Torridge Valley. Descend steeply; where the track bears left bear right over a stile into woodland. Follow the narrow path downhill along the bottom edge of th wood to then bear right along the Torridge, crossing a footbridge on rou (and a memorial seat at a good rivers picnic spot). The path rises away from the river to pass behind Beaford Mill

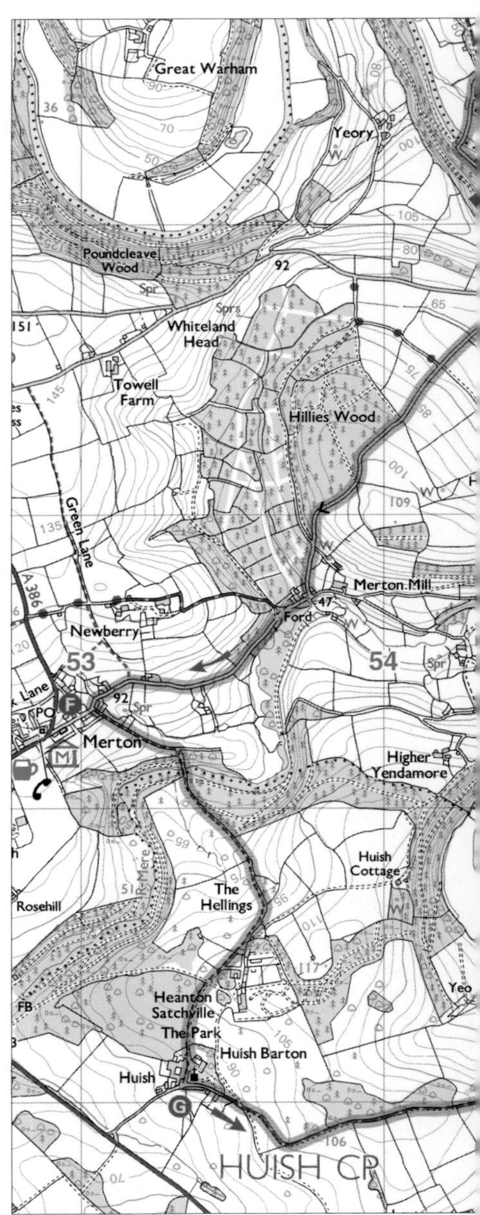

House and climbs steadily to meet a lane.

Turn left downhill **D** past Beaford Mill (dated 1867) and cross Beaford Bridge. Follow the lane down valley, bearing right to a lane junction at Balls Corner. Take the left fork **E** signed Merton 1¼ miles and follow this quiet lane between flower-filled hedgebanks to climb steadily past Hillies Wood before dropping steeply to a junction at Merton Mill Cross. Turn right; the lane ascends to reach cottages on the edge of

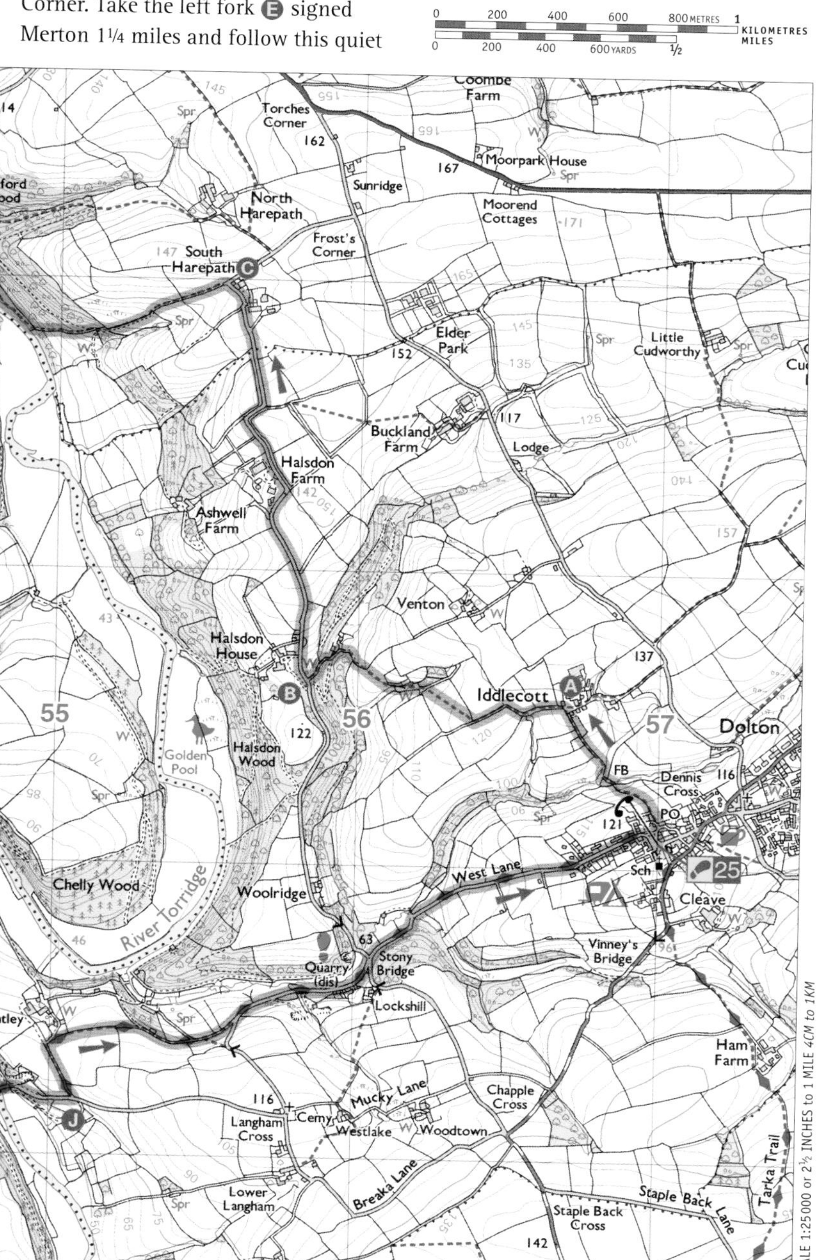

The Torridge from Beaford Bridge

Merton. Just past The Old Smithy (left) turn left F *(for the* **Malt Scoop Inn** *keep straight ahead along the lane to the A386 and turn left)* on a footpath that follows a green lane downhill to pass through woodland (wet underfoot). Cross the River Mere and through a gate into parkland. Follow a grassy track steadily up the left edge, eventually to pass through a gate onto a concrete drive; bear right. At a crossroads of drives keep ahead downhill between iron park railings; look back left to see Heanton Satchville. The ancestral home of the Yeo family for several hundred years, the estate is now owned by Lord Clinton, a Yeo descendant: the present building was built in 1935 to replace a late 18th-century mansion, which was gutted by fire. Pass old farm buildings at Huish Barton and meet a lane.

Turn left G to pass the Church of St James the Less, which Lord Clinton had extensively restored in the late 19th century; many Clinton family members are buried in the churchyard. He also had a school built here in 1847.

Follow the lane past the Old Rectory and through a gate. Re-enter the park; at a junction keep ahead gently uphill on a concrete way, with a fence left. Pass through a gate, then bear left on a track which runs pleasantly along the top edge of fields, with views right to Dartmoor. Pass through a small strip of woodland and keep ahead on the track, soon dropping gently. Where it bears sharp left keep straight ahead across the field to pass through a gate into woodland; continue downhill to pass through a gate. Bear right past cottages to reach a lane via another gate.

Turn left H (Tarka Trail) to cross New Bridge over the Torridge. Follow the lane steeply uphill past a quarry; turn left J where signed on a driveway to reach a junction. Turn right through an open gateway and walk along the left edge of a field. On meeting the wire fence at the end turn right across the field to pass over a stile onto a narrow fenced path. Cross another stile; follow the track gently downhill through woodland to meet a lane.

Turn left and follow the lane downhill to Woolridge Cross, then steadily uphill into Dolton to find The Square on the right.

Sandford, Shobrooke & Upton Hellions

Start	Sandford
Distance	11½ miles (18.3km)
Height gain	1,395 feet (425m)
Approximate time	5½ hours
Parking	Parish Hall car park, Sandford (free); Sandford is 1½ miles north of Crediton, signed off A3072
Route terrain	Undulating fields, woodland, parkland, lanes; brief road stretch through Crediton; muddy tracks through Trew Woods
Dog friendly	To be kept on leads through parkland and farmland
Ordnance Survey maps	Landranger 191 (Okehampton & North Dartmoor), Explorer 114 (Exeter & the Exe Valley)

GPS waypoints

- SS 830 025
- A SS 836 001
- B SS 860 011
- C SS 872 014
- D SS 867 029
- E SS 862 033
- F SS 857 038
- G SS 851 033
- H SS 844 023
- J SS 839 032

This is a real leg-stretcher through rolling 'Redland' countryside, with big skies and far-reaching views. The route clips the edge of Crediton via Devon's first cathedral, and visits three delightful rural churches. Keep a close eye on footpath arrows through Trew Wood. Note that many field-edge paths are rough underfoot and that in summer arable crops may necessitate field-edge walking.

Turn left; at the T-junction cross into the churchyard of St Swithun, built on the site of a Saxon chapel. Take the second path left onto Church Lane; turn right for The Square (**Lamb Inn**, 16th-century posting house). Turn left past the PO/Community Stores. At the road continue downhill past the **Rose & Crown**; at the next corner turn right through a gate. Follow the community path to Crediton, crossing a road and zigzagging uphill through woodland to Higher Road. Cross over; turn left to Forches Cross.

Turn sharp right down Deep Lane. At the T-junction (Town Square/**Three Little Pigs** right) keep ahead down a tarmac way (library left) into Newcombe's Meadow. Turn left; the path winds through the park to reach Church Lane. Turn right, soon entering the churchyard of the Church of the Holy Cross; the missionary St Boniface was born here in AD680, and a cathedral established in AD909; the see moved to Exeter in AD1050 when St Peter's Cathedral was consecrated. Bear right at the south door to reach East Street.

Turn left (A); where the main road bears right keep ahead. At the T-junction turn left, soon passing the **Crediton Inn**. The road bears right; turn

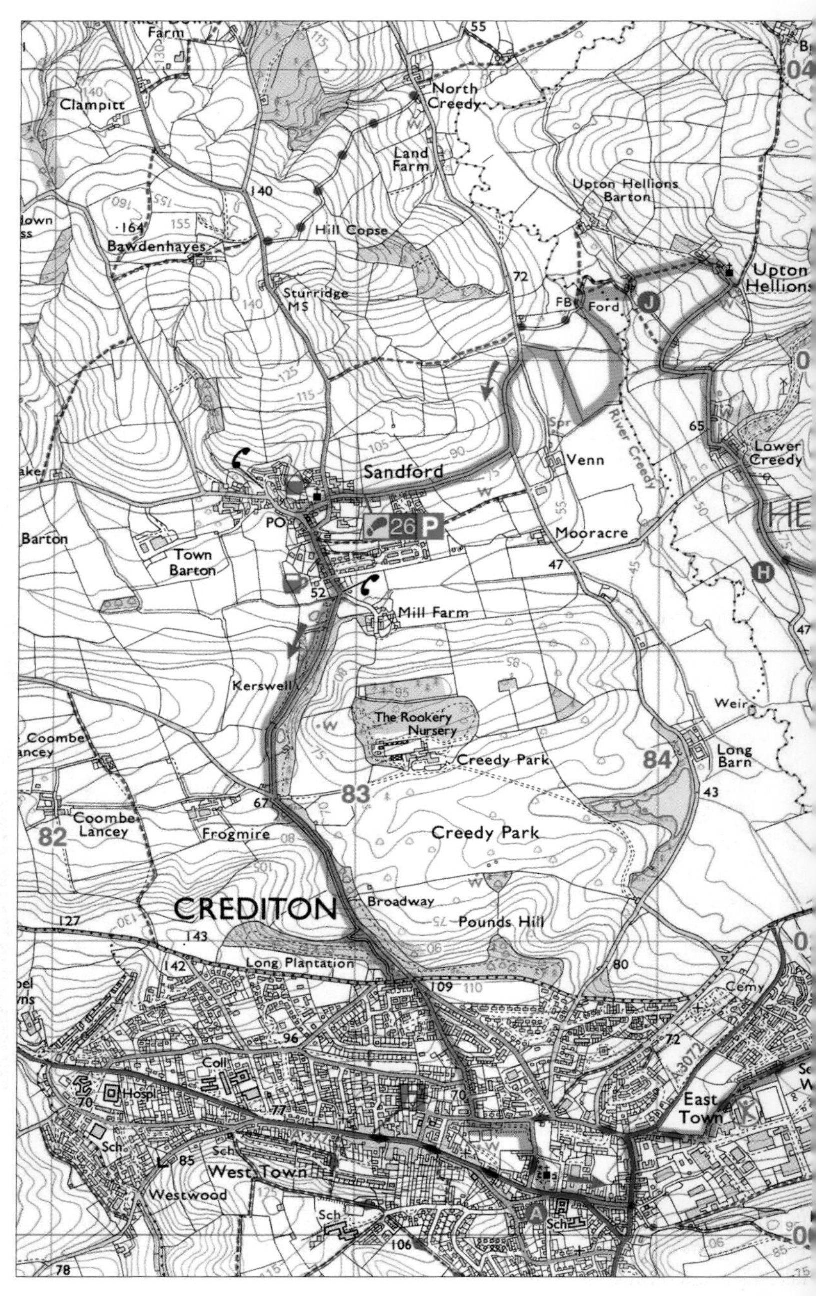

right on Commercial Road (Devonshire Heartland Way DHW). Turn left past the Sports Centre; take the path left of the car park and along the left edge of Lord's Meadow. Cross a stream (footbridge) and head across the field. Cross Mill Leat (footbridge) and cross the next field to a lane via a kissing-gate.

Turn left for 300 yds; turn sharp right into Shobrooke Park *(occasionally in midsummer this path is temporarily closed: retrace your steps and follow the*

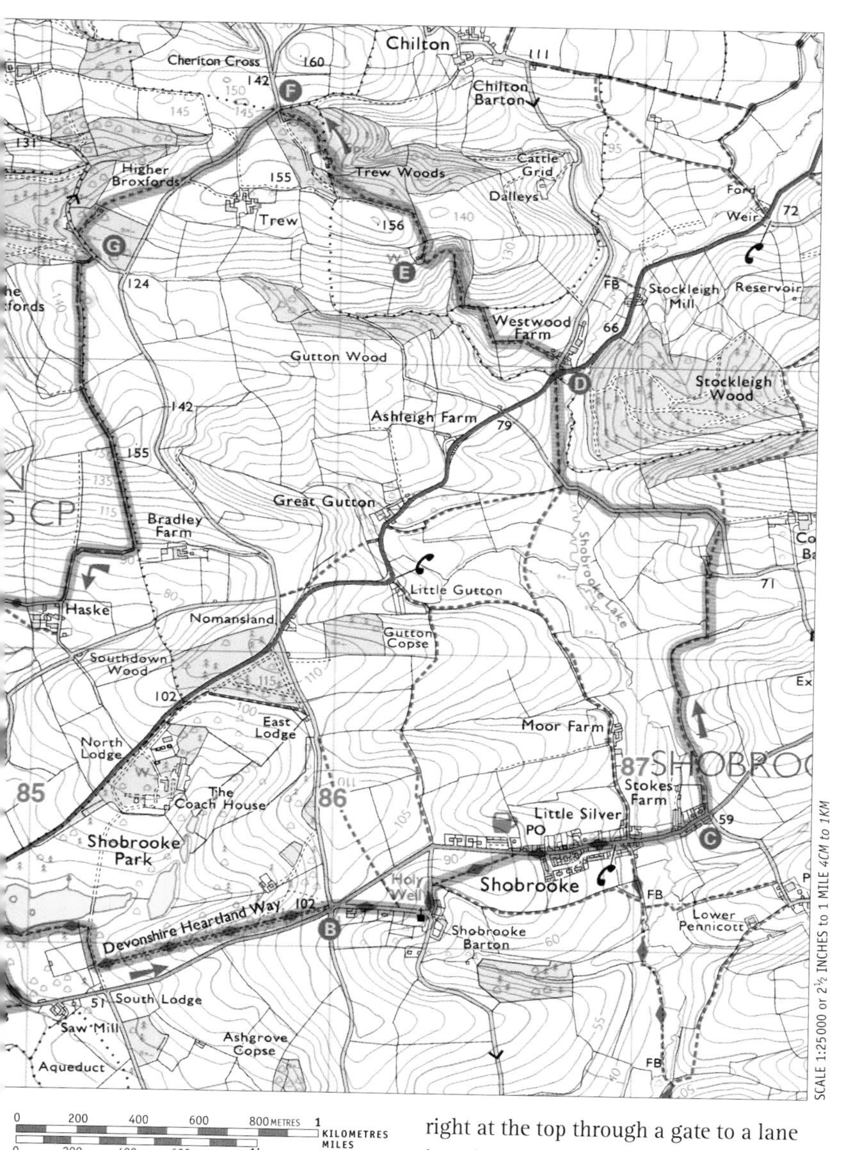

lane to B*)*. Bear half right, aiming for a fence corner; bear left along the lakeside. Pass through a kissing-gate in a fence to meet a track; turn right past the cricket pitch; on meeting a gate (South Lodge ahead) turn left up a lime tree avenue – views to the coach house and walled garden left (the main house was destroyed by fire in 1947) – bearing right at the top through a gate to a lane junction.

Turn left to Shobrooke Cross, then bear right B downhill to St Swithun's Church (which has a medieval exterior with a Norman doorway). The lane bears right; turn left, then right over a stile. The DHW bears diagonally left uphill across the field, through a gate onto the lane opposite Shobrooke (from 'sheep-' or 'trout-' brook) village hall.

Turn right downhill past **The Red**

Lion. Cross Shobrooke Lake (stream); where houses end turn left Ⓒ through a gate. Follow the right edge of two fields. Follow the left edge of the next, which curves right; after 100 yds turn left through a gate and up the left field edge to a gate; turn right to a track. Cross a stile ahead; ascend the left edge of the field to meet a lane via a gate.

Turn left. Descend to cross Shobrooke Lake (ford after heavy rainfall); just round the bend turn right over a stile. The right of way heads straight across the field, aiming for farm buildings, to cross a stile onto the A3072 Ⓓ.

Cross with care; walk up the lane opposite. At Westwood Farm (past a big open-fronted barn left) turn left through a gate on an uphill track. Pass through a gate (muddy) at the top; follow the hedge right to pass through a gate in the top corner into woodland. Emerge into a field via a gate. The signed footpath here is overgrown; drop left to hit clearer grassland and continue uphill towards a small wooden building. Meet a path level with it and turn left; follow the left fork round the slope and climb to a gate, with a house left Ⓔ. Keep up the track for 100 yds; bear right into woodland. Bear left at the next arrow onto a track; at the next footpath post keep ahead. Turn right at the next and descend steeply downhill to a track; turn left uphill, passing a house, eventually to reach a lane.

Turn left Ⓕ; opposite Trew House bear right through a gate. Aim for the far corner (right of a telegraph pole) and cross a stile; keep ahead to reach a lane. Turn left; after 200 yds turn right Ⓖ on a bridleway, which soon bears left along the edge of rolling fields with stunning views. The track drops steeply to Bradley Farm; turn right across fields to reach Haske Farm on a corner. Keep ahead on a hedged track and descend to a lane.

Turn right Ⓗ, eventually climbing to a T-junction. Turn left past St Mary's simple church at Upton Hellions, dating from the 12th century and now little used. The lane leads through entrance gates; keep ahead through a gate into a field, with a house right. Bear left downhill through a gate in a fence; bear left downhill and through another onto a track. Turn left to the Old Mill.

Turn right in front of the mill Ⓙ; just past the pond turn left through a gate, then bear right across the field to a gate onto a track. Bear left to cross a footbridge over the Creedy. Meet a track; keep ahead through a gate and riverside meadows to cross a footbridge; turn left along a fenced path. Bear right through a gate and along the left edge of a field to pass through another. Turn right along the bottom of the next (wet underfoot), keeping the hedge on the right all the way round to a gate onto a lane; turn left. Just over the brow of the hill turn right at Fanny's Lane to Sandford. ●

Looking back across the fields to Shobrooke church

Hartland Point & Speke's Mill Mouth

Start	Rocket House, Hartland Quay
Distance	10½ miles (16.6km)
Height gain	2,230 feet (680m)
Approximate time	6 hours
Parking	Extensive parking area (£2 charge in high season 2010) above Hartland Quay, 2½ miles west of Hartland village
Route terrain	Strenuous Coast Path with many steep ascents and descents: inland route undulating green lanes and tracks
Dog friendly	To be kept on leads through fields
Ordnance Survey maps	Landranger 180 (Barnstaple & Ilfracombe), Explorer 139 (Bideford, Ilfracombe & Barnstaple)

GPS waypoints	
Start	SS 226 247
A	SS 230 266
B	SS 233 275
C	SS 235 273
D	SS 232 262
E	SS 235 246
F	SS 231 218
G	SS 223 218
H	SS 227 233
J	SS 223 246

The remote Hartland peninsula – Ptolemy's 'Promontory of Hercules' – is Devon's most northwesterly point, and holds the toughest section of the South West Coast Path. This route encounters a succession of steep-sided combes, rocky bays and magnificent coastal scenery – and a wonderful feeling of space. Inland green lanes provide pleasant walking past Hartland Abbey and Docton Mill, perfectly placed for tea.

From the car park entrance (toll booth) pass through a gate by the Rocket House. Follow the Coast Path along the cliffs *(take care)* above Hartland Quay, dating from 1586 – when inland communications were almost non-existent – and active until the late 19th century when the quay was destroyed by the sea. Descend into the valley, turning inland to a junction; turn left across the Abbey River. Pass behind Blackpool Mill Cottage (location for the TV drama *Sense & Sensibility*) to a track.

Turn left then climb very steeply right uphill (steps). At the top pass through a gate and turn right, bearing left at the next post along Blegberry Cliff: the contorted rocks along this coast are a geologist's dream. Descend across a stile and head downhill. The path drops rockily to cross a stream in a steep-sided flower-filled gorge above Blegberry beach. Ascend steeply; soon descend into Smoothlands via an eroded path. At the end of the valley rise to a footpath junction and follow the left edge of a big field, eventually passing through a gate; follow the Coast Path left **A** at the next junction.

Descend uneven steps into the next combe; cross a stream before bearing

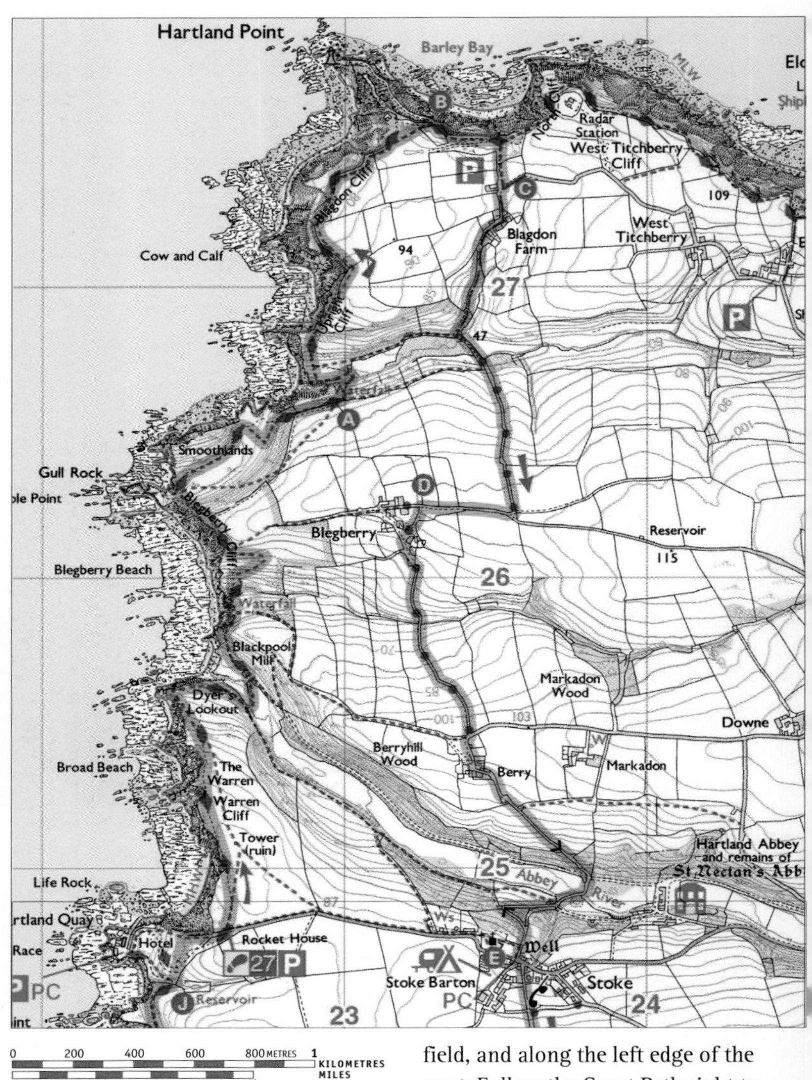

back to the coast. At the next post bear right to climb steeply onto Upright Cliff, eventually with a wire fence right. The path levels on Blagdon Cliff. Where the wire fence ends bear left along the cliff edge, passing through gorse and along the left edge of the next field: a memorial (left) to the torpedoed *Glenart Castle* affords views over Hartland Point lighthouse (erected 1874) and, on a clear day, to Lundy. Continue up the field, and along the left edge of the next. Follow the Coast Path right to meet a track by the lighthouse gates.

Turn right **B** through a parking area at Shipload Bay, passing the **café** (seasonal); bear right up the access road past Lundy's helicopter terminal. Where the road bears sharp left keep ahead **C** to descend through Blagdon Farm. The track passes through a gate and continues downhill along the right edge of a field, and through another gate. Meet a junction; turn left to cross a stream into woodland. Cross a footbridge and walk steadily up a green lane to reach a broad track, and bear left; eventually pass through a gate, bearing right to a lane. Turn right.

At the entrance to Blegberry Farm turn left **D** (unsigned) down a drive. Where that bears right keep ahead on a green lane that descends steeply then rises to pass through a big gate to meet a lane on a corner; keep straight ahead past buildings at Berry. Descend into the Abbey Valley, with views to Hartland Abbey (dating from 1157: the present house was rebuilt in 1779); climb steeply uphill into Stoke by St Nectan's church with its landmark 128ft tower, the highest in Devon (toilets). *Note that cream teas are available at* **Stoke Barton** *a few yards to the right.*

Turn left **E**; almost immediately turn right (by Church House) on a tarmac lane. Where it bears sharp left follow the broad green lane ahead into and out of a valley to reach Wargery Farm; turn right on the farm drive to a lane junction at Kernstone Cross. Follow the lane ahead, dropping steeply to the crossroads at Lymebridge. Keep straight on (Docton Mill and Gardens right, **tearoom**) steeply uphill, levelling off

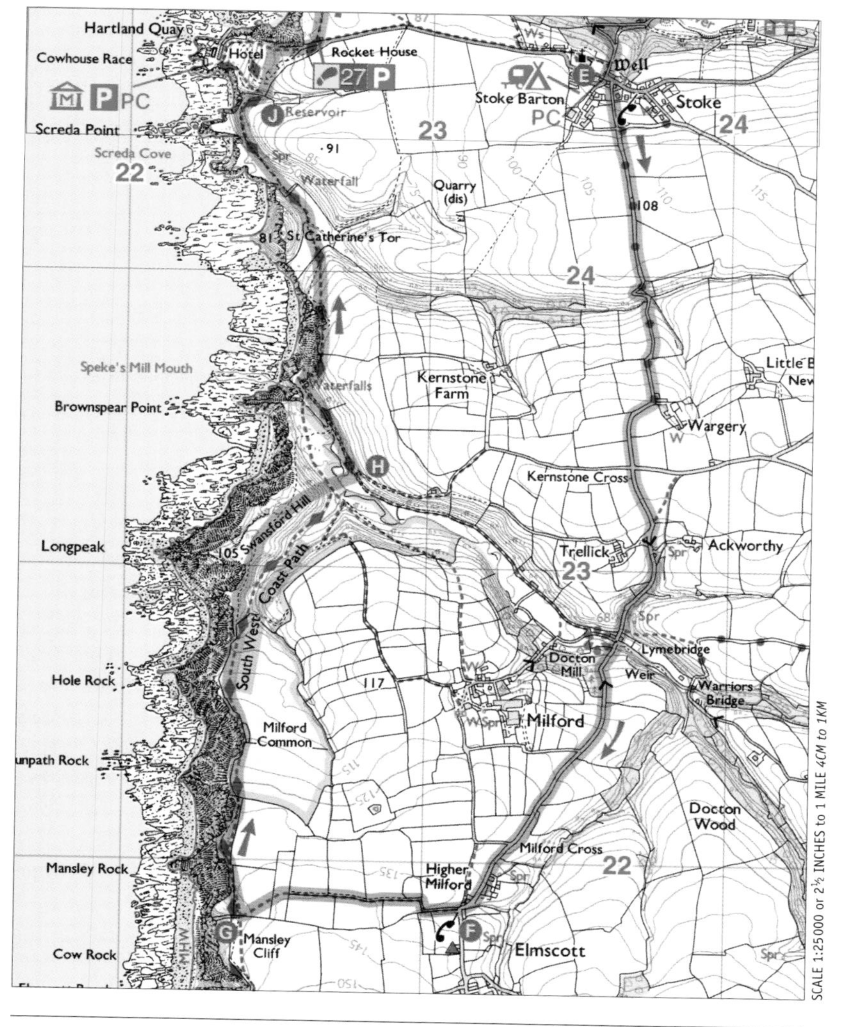

and passing Milford Cross. Pass Lower Elmscott Farm; where the lane bears sharp left, with Post Box Cottage right, keep ahead on a signed concrete way F.

The hedged track eventually passes along the left edge of fields and through a gateway into a field. Bear diagonally left, aiming for the far corner, and through a gate onto the Coast Path.

Turn right G along massive cliffs. Pass through a gate and along the seaward edge of a wire fence *(precipitous)*; cross a stile and go through a gate, soon passing a bench on the cliff edge. Cross a stile; soon meet a post, with the Coast Path signed right (valley route), but keep ahead on the cliff-top path over Swansford Hill, with a deep valley right. Towards the end of the hill wonderful views of steep-sided St Catherine's Tor and Hartland Quay appear ahead. The path starts to descend along a narrow ridge *(take care)*; look right to spot a Coast Path post on the track in the valley. Drop right and aim for that post, picking up another en route where the Coast Paths re-joins; turn left across the stream on a footbridge, and ascend to the track.

Turn left H and follow the track towards Speke's Mill Mouth; note the waterfall left. At the next Coast Path post turn right to zigzag steeply out of the combe to pass through a gate. Descend, soon bearing inland to pass through a gate. Walk towards the right edge of St Catherine's Tor; cross a stream on stepping stones and bear left to pass through a hedgebank gap. Keep ahead to find a rising track, which bears left round the hill; pass through a gate, then walk left towards Hartland Quay. At the next Coast Path post J turn left for the Quay and **hotel**; to complete the walk keep ahead across the parking area to meet a lane. Cross over; turn right to find the Coast Path, which rises steeply to the Rocket House.

Hartland Point lighthouse

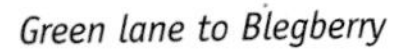

Green lane to Blegberry

Countryside Access Charter

Your rights of way are:

- public footpaths – on foot only. Sometimes waymarked in yellow
- bridle-ways – on foot, horseback and pedal cycle. Sometimes waymarked in blue
- byways (usually old roads), most 'roads used as public paths' and, of course, public roads – all traffic has the right of way

Use maps, signs and waymarks to check rights of way. Ordnance Survey Explorer and Landranger maps show most public rights of way

On rights of way you can:

- take a pram, pushchair or wheelchair if practicable
- take a dog (on a lead or under close control)
- take a short route round an illegal obstruction or remove it sufficiently to get past

You have a right to go for recreation to:

- public parks and open spaces – on foot
- most commons near older towns and cities – on foot and sometimes on horseback
- private land where the owner has a formal agreement with the local authority

In addition you can use the following by local or established custom or consent, but ask for advice if you are unsure:

- many areas of open country, such as moorland, fell and coastal areas, especially those in the care of the National Trust, and some commons
- some woods and forests, especially those owned by the Forestry Commission
- country parks and picnic sites
- most beaches
- canal towpaths
- some private paths and tracks Consent sometimes extends to horse-riding and cycling

For your information:

- county councils and London boroughs maintain and record rights of way, and register commons
- obstructions, dangerous animals, harassment and misleading signs on rights of way are illegal and you should report them to the county council
- paths across fields can be ploughed, but must normally be reinstated within two weeks
- landowners can require you to leave land to which you have no right of access
- motor vehicles are normally permitted only on roads, byways and some 'roads used as public paths'

and estate roads, although occasionally they will be found crossing mountainous area.

Rights of way are marked on Ordnance Survey maps. Look for the green broken lines on the Explorer maps, or the red dashed lines on Landranger maps.

The term 'right of way' means exactly what it says. It gives a right of passage over what, for the most part, is private land. Under pre-CRoW legislation walkers were required to keep to the line of the right of way and not stray onto land on either side. If you did inadvertently wander off the right of way, either because of faulty map reading or because the route was not clearly indicated on the ground, you were technically trespassing.

Local authorities have a legal obligation to ensure that rights of way are kept clear and free of obstruction, and are signposted where they leave metalled roads. The duty of local authorities to install signposts extends to the placing of signs along a path or way, but only where the authority considers it necessary to have a signpost or waymark to assist persons unfamiliar with the locality.

The New Access Rights

Access Land

As well as being able to walk on existing rights of way, under the new legislation you now have access to large areas of open land. You can of course continue to use rights of way footpaths to cross this land, but the main difference is that you can now lawfully leave the path and wander at will, but only in areas designated as access land.

Where to Walk
Areas now covered by the new access rights – Access Land – are shown on Ordnance  Survey Explorer maps bearing the access land symbol on the front cover.

'Access Land' is shown on Ordnance Survey maps by a light yellow tint surrounded by a pale orange border. New orange coloured 'i' symbols on the maps will show the location of permanent access information boards installed by the access authorities.

Restrictions
The right to walk on access land may lawfully be restricted by landowners. Landowners can, for any reason, restrict access for up to 28 days in any year. They cannot however close the land:

- on bank holidays;
- for more than four Saturdays and Sundays in a year;
- on any Saturday from 1 June to 11 August; or
- on any Sunday from 1 June to the end of September.

They have to provide local authorities with five working days' notice before the date of closure unless the land involved is an area of less than five hectares or the closure is for less than four hours. In these cases landowners only need to provide two hours' notice.

Whatever restrictions are put into place on access land they have no effect on existing rights of way, and you can continue to walk on them.

Dogs
Dogs can be taken on access land, but must be kept on leads of two metres or less between 1 March and 31 July, and at all times where they are near livestock. In addition landowners may impose a ban on all dogs from fields where lambing takes place for up to six weeks in any year. Dogs may be banned from moorland used for grouse shooting and breeding for up to five years.

In the main, walkers following the routes in this book will continue to follow existing rights of way, but a knowledge and understanding of the law as it affects walkers, plus the ability to distinguish access land marked on the maps, will enable anyone who wishes to depart from paths that cross access land either to take a shortcut, to enjoy a view or to explore.

General Obstructions
Obstructions can sometimes cause a problem on a walk and the most common of these is where the path across a field has been ploughed over. It is legal for a farmer to plough up a path provided that it is restored within two weeks. This does not always happen and you are faced with the dilemma of following the line of the path, even if this means treading on crops, or walking round the edge of the field. Although the latter course of action seems the most sensible, it does mean that you would be trespassing.

Other obstructions can vary from overhanging vegetation to wire fences across the path, locked gates or even a cattle feeder on the path.

Use common sense. If you can get round the obstruction without causing damage, do so. Otherwise only remove as much of the obstruction as is necessary to secure passage.

If the right of way is blocked and cannot be followed, there is a long-standing view that in such circumstances there is a right to deviate, but this cannot wholly be relied on. Although it is accepted in law that highways (and that includes rights of way) are for the public service, and if the usual track is impassable, it is for the general good that people should be entitled to pass into another line. However, this should not be taken as indicating a right to deviate whenever a way is impassable. If in doubt, retreat.

Report obstructions to the local authority and/or the Ramblers.

Useful Organisations

Campaign to Protect Rural England
CPRE National Office
128 Southwark St, London SE1 0SW

Tel. 020 7981 2800
www.cpre.org.uk

English Heritage
Customer Services, PO Box 569,
Swindon SN2 2YP
Tel. 0870 333 1181
www.english-heritage.org.uk

Forestry Commission
Bank House, Bank Street, Coleford,
Gloucestershire GL16 8BA
Tel. 01594 833 057
www.forestry.gov.uk

Independent Hostels
The Backpackers Press, Speedwell House,
Upperwood, Matlock Bath DE4 3PE
Tel. 01629 580 427
www.IndependentHostelsUK.co.uk

Lundy Island Shore Office
Tel. 01271 863636
www.lundyisland.co.uk

The National Trust
Devon Regional Office
Killerton House, Broadclyst, Exeter EX5 3LE
Tel. 01392 881691
Membership and general enquiries
PO Box 39, Warrington WA5 7WD
Tel. 0870 458 4000
www.nationaltrust.org.uk

Natural England
John Dower House, Crescent Place,
Cheltenham GL50 3RA
Tel. 0300 060 2481
www.naturalengland.org.uk

Ramblers
2nd Floor, Camelford House, 87–90
Albert Embankment, London SE1 7TW
Tel. 0207 339 8500
www.ramblers.org.uk

Youth Hostels Association
Trevelyan House, Dimple Road,
Matlock DE4 3YH
Tel. 0870 770 8868
www.yha.org.uk

Traveline: 0871 200 2233
National train enquiry line: 08457 484950

Tourist Information
Exmoor National Park Authority
Exmoor House, Dulverton, Somerset
TA22 9HL
Tel. 01398 323 665
email info@exmoor-nationalpark.gov.uk
www.exmoor-nationalpark.gov.uk

Tourist Information Centres
Barnstaple: 01271 375 000
Bideford: 01237 477 676
Braunton: 01271 816 400
Combe Martin (ENPA): 01271 883 319
Dulverton (ENPA): 01398 323841
Dunster (ENPA) 01643 821835
Great Torrington: 01805 626 140
Holsworthy: 01409 254 185
Ilfracombe: 01271 863 001
Lynton & Lynmouth: 0845 603 232
Okehampton: 01837 53020
South Molton: 01769 574 122
Tiverton: 01884 255 827
Woolacombe: 01271 870 553

Ordnance Survey maps of North Devon

North Devon is covered by Ordnance Survey 1:50 000 scale (1¼ inches to 1 mile or 2cm to 1km) Landranger map sheets 180, 181, 190, 191 and 192. These all-purpose maps are packed with information to help you explore the area. Viewpoints, picnic sites, places of interest and caravan and camping sites are shown, as well as public rights of way information such as footpaths and bridleways. To examine North Devon in more detail, and especially if you are planning walks, Ordnance Survey Explorer maps at 1:25 000 (2½ inches to 1 mile or 4cm to 1km) are ideal:

OL9 Exmoor
112 Launceston & Holsworthy
113 Okehampton
114 Exeter & the Exe Valley
126 Clovelly & Hartland
127 South Molton & Chulmleigh
139 Bideford, Ilfracombe & Barnstaple

To get to North Devon, use the Ordnance Survey Travel Map-Route Great Britain at 1:625 000 (1 inch to 10 miles or 4cm to 25km) scale.